CHINESE WISDOM AND PHILOSOPHY THROUGH THE AGES

ISBN 978-0-578-93583-6

Library of Congress Control Number: 2021912337

Book design by Longworth Creative, LLC.
www.LongworthCreative.com

First Edition

Printed in the United States of America

CHINESE WISDOM AND PHILOSOPHY THROUGH THE AGES

PROVERBS FROM THE MING DYNASTY

Ken Kuang, Runyu Ye, Yanjun Cheng
and Jenny Tripp

TORREY HILLS TECHNOLOGIES, LLC

San Diego, CA

前言
PREFACE

今天的炎黄子孙在世界的每一个角落几乎都可以找到，而且都是当地社会的佼佼者。炎黄子孙为何能在全世界兴旺？为何全世界的中国人，不管他们离开中国这块土地多少年，都不约而同的注重教育，勤俭持家，诚实守信，自强不息，尊老爱幼等。中国人没有圣经，但祖先给留下了很多文化瑰宝，《增广贤文》是其中之一。

Today's Chinese can be found in almost every corner of the world, and they are very productive members in local societies. How do Chinese prosper all over the world? Overseas Chinese people, no matter how many years / generations they have left the land of China, always value education, hard work, thrifty lifestyles, honesty and trustworthiness, continuous self-improvement, respect for the old and love for the young, etc. Chinese ancestors have left many cultural treasures behind. "Chinese Wisdom and Philosophy Through the Ages" is one of them.

《增广贤文》，又名《昔时贤文》《古今贤文》，是中国明代时期编写的儿童启蒙书目。书名最早见之于明万历年间的戏曲《牡丹亭》，据此可推知此书最迟写成于万历年间。

"Chinese Wisdom and Philosophy Through the Ages," also known as "Ancient Wisdom and Philosophy" and "Wisdom and Philosophy in Ancient and Modern Times," is a children's enlightenment book compiled during the Ming Dynasty in China (1573 – 1620). The title of the book was first seen in the opera "Peony Pavilion" during the Wanli period of the Ming Dynasty, because of this it can be inferred that this book was written during the Wanli period at the latest.

《增广贤文》集结中国从古到今的各种格言、谚语。后来，经过明、清两代文人的不断增补，才改成现在这个模样，称《增广昔时贤文》，通称《增广贤文》。作者一直未见任何书载，只知道清代同治年间儒生周希陶曾进行过重订。

"Chinese Wisdom and Philosophy Through the Ages" gathers various Chinese sayings and proverbs from ancient times to the present. Later, after the scholars from the Ming and Qing dynasties continued to revise it, then it was changed to its current form. The real author has never been mentioned in any of the ancient books. It was known that Zhou Xitao, a Confucian scholar during the Tongzhi period of the Qing Dynasty (1862–1874), had re-edited it.

我们兄妹4人和这本书的根源能追溯到上世纪70年代。在江西农村，很小的时候，我们的父亲况俊福就会给我们讲这本书，教导我们如何做人。40 多年过去了，书中的教诲一直在潜移默化地影响我们的学习、生活和事业。

Our love for this book can be traced back to the 1970s. In rural Jiangxi, when we were young, our father Kuang, Junfu would tell us this book and teach us how to be decent human beings. More than 40 years have passed, and the teachings in the book are still subtly affecting all of our lives.

我们发现这本书中的道理非常地深奥。从某种意义上来说，它包含了中国三个古典哲学思想佛教、道教和儒家三派精华汇总：

1) 佛家的人生观和轮回观
2) 道教的辩证思维
3) 儒家的"中庸之道"。不偏不倚，合乎中道

We found the teachings in this book to be very profound. In a sense, it contains the essence of the three schools of Chinese classical philosophy: Buddhism, Taoism and Confucianism:

1) Buddhist outlook on life and reincarnation
2) Daoist dialectical thinking
3) Confucian "The Doctrine of the Mean"

有几点，我们的感触特别深：

1) **做人之道** - 贤文里面讲，害人之心不可有，防人之心不可无！有时候是这样的。比如在商场上，如果你不采取非常手段，自己会添麻烦，一但别人要压制你，人家也是会用这种手段。在战场上，不要光认为，举手投降的俘虏不可杀。一旦他们利用你的怜悯之心，他反过来用奸诈的计谋将你杀了。你还能讲"害人之心不可有"吗？一定要有"防人之心不可无"。貌似对立，其实后面是统一的。最高的观点，让大家，利用这种文明，最高境界的生存，不要害人家的性命和人家的钱财。但一定要记住最原始的丛林法则。为人处世可以学习，丛林法则不要忘。

2) **自立自强** - 人在社会上生存，应该自强自立，做事讲究天时地利人和，凡事顺天意。要强大，也要明白自己。在自强自立的基础上，多种花少种刺，赠人玫瑰，手留余香。

3) **敬畏自然** - 不可以违背大自然规律，正所谓谋事在人，成事在天！顺天者昌，逆天者亡。

4) **普及爱心** - 在自强自立的基础上，随时准备帮助有真正需要的人。老吾老人之老，幼吾幼以及人之幼。爱人者，人恒爱。敬人者，人恒敬。

5) **吃亏是福** - 吃得亏，坐一堆；要得好，大做小。近看是吃亏，远看是大福。我们人有时候要吃自己的饭去给人家割水稻，首先得有事做，才能有机会将才华展现给他人。

Specifically, we felt very strongly on the passages:

1) **How to be a decent human being:** As stated in the book that Harmfulness is not allowed, and defensiveness is necessary! For example, in the business world, we should always learn to trust people; at the same time, we make sure that our positions are defendable. On the battlefield, we should show leniency towards captured prisoners of war; at the same time, be mindful they may still be able to hurt you. This is a classic example of the Unity of Opposite. It seems to be opposite, but in fact, both positions can be reconciled. The ultimate goal is not to harm other people's lives and other people's property. But we must remember the most primitive law of the jungle (survival of the fittest).

2) **Self-reliance:** People should be self-reliant in order to survive and thrive in the long term. To be strong, but also to understand

yourself. With self-reliance in mind, one should always be ready to assist those who are in real need.

3) **Respect for nature:** Do not violate the laws of nature. Those who follow the nature's law will prosper, and those who go against the nature's law will suffer.

4) **Universal love:** While focusing on self-reliance, one should always be ready to help others in real need. Love other's elders and children as your own.

5) **Short term Suffering is a blessing:** A person who is willing to accept losses can make many friends and win a network of resources; if a person wants to be affirmed by others, he must lower his posture and respect others. In business very often we are willing to accept some short loss happily, so we have an opportunity to show our talents to others.

《增广贤文》包含很多深奥的人生哲理，在翻译的过程中，况秀猛和整个团队尽力在考虑相应历史背景下，将它的意思表达出来。由于时间仓促和水平有限，一定有不到之处。期待读者能够理解和包含不周之处，不吝赐教，能在下一版中改进。共同来将中华民族的智慧分享给全世界。 谢谢！

"Chinese Wisdom and Philosophy Through the Ages" book has many profound life wisdoms that are very hard to translate. During the translation process, Kuang, Xiumeng (Ken) and the whole team tried their best to interpret their meanings in the context of the corresponding historical background. Due to the limited time and resources, there may be some inaccuracies. We hope that readers can share their feedback and help improve the translation in the next edition. Together let's share the wisdom and life philosophies of the Chinese with the world. Thank you!

况秀勇，况秀莲，况秀猛和况秀清, 2021年6月

Xiuyong Kuang, Xiulian Kuang, Xiumeng (Ken) Kuang and Xiuqing Kuang

June 2021

A very old copy of 《增广贤文》

《增广贤文》 *by Ai Guangqin*

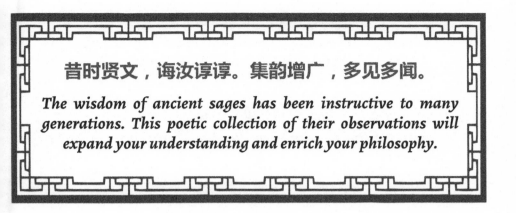

昔时贤文，诲汝谆谆。集韵增广，多见多闻。

The wisdom of ancient sages has been instructive to many generations. This poetic collection of their observations will expand your understanding and enrich your philosophy.

观今宜鉴古，无古不成今。

Knowing history is invaluable in understanding the present, because history determines what the present will look like.

知己知彼，将心比心。

Know both yourself and others; feel for both yourself and others.

酒逢知己饮，诗向会人吟。相识满天下，知心能几人。

Savor good wine and chant poetry with your confidantes. Nodding acquaintances are everywhere, but true confidantes are rare.

相逢好似初相识，到老终无怨恨心。

Every reunion is as if the friends meet for the first time, and there are no resentments until the day's end.

近水知鱼性，近山识鸟音。

To know the nature of fish, go to the water; to learn the songs of birds, go to the mountains.

易涨易退山溪水，易反易覆小人心。

Quick to rise and recede is the mountain flash flood. Quick to chop and change is the villain's mind.

运去金成铁，时来铁似金。

Misfortune turns gold into iron; good luck turns iron into gold.

逢人且说三分话，未可全抛一片心。

All truths are not to be told.

有意栽花花不发，无心插柳柳成荫。

Flowers well cared for may grow no blossoms, but willows left in disrepair grow into shade.

画虎画皮难画骨，知人知面不知心。

It's as hard to draw its skeleton when painting a tiger as it is to see into a man's mind when getting to know him.

钱财如粪土，仁义值千金。

Wealth and riches are dust, but righteousness is beyond price.

流水下滩非有意，白云出岫本无心。

The waves upon the beach move without meaning. The clouds that float from the cave are unconscious.

当时若不登高望，谁信东流海洋深。

If you haven't looked down at it from the mountain top, how can you comprehend the ocean's depth?

路遥知马力，日久见人心。

Distance tests a horse's stamina. Time reveals a man's heart.

相见易得好，久住难为人。

It's easy to become close on the first meeting, but hard to get along well over a long time.

美不美，乡中水；亲不亲，故乡人。

Delicious is the water from our hometown; close are the people of our hometown.

读书须用意，一字值千金。

Study diligently, so that your one word is worth a thousand dollars.

马行无力皆因瘦，人不风流只为贫。

The weakness of a horse is due to thinness, and the boring routine of a man is due to poorness.

饶人不是痴汉，痴汉不会饶人。

Kind people with forgiving hearts are not idiots; idiots will not treat people kindly.

是亲不是亲，非亲却是亲。

"Blood kin" doesn't mean close, and "unrelated tie" doesn't mean distant.

莺花犹怕春光老，岂可教人枉度春。

Passing spring doesn't wait for a warbler; wasting time drains
a man.

两人一般心，无钱堪买金；一人一般心，有钱难买针。

Buy gold with no money when two people unite with one heart
and one mind. Buy not so much as a needle with much money
when each of them has his own axe to grind.

相逢不饮空归去，洞口桃花也笑人。

When good friends meet without enjoying a drink together,
even the peach blossoms droop in disappointment.

红粉佳人休使老，风流浪子莫教贫。

Let beauties stay young, let lads make their fortunes.

在家不会迎宾客，出门方知少主人。

If you don't serve guests at your home, no one will serve you
when you go out.

黄芩（金）无假，阿魏无真。

There is no fake rock but there is no real diamond.

客来主不顾，自是无良宾。

If a host ignores guests, they won't be good guests.

良宾主不顾，应恐是痴人。

If a host ignores nice guests, the host is an idiot.

贫居闹市无人问，富在深山有远亲。

No one cares about a poor friend who lives across town, but they'll cross far mountains to visit rich acquaintances.

谁人背后无人说，哪个人前不说人。

No one escapes backstabbing; everyone talks behind other's back.

有钱道真语，无钱语不真。

When one is rich and powerful, one's word counts; otherwise, whatever one says doesn't matter much.

不信但看筵中酒，杯杯先劝有钱人。

Observe the rule of toasting at a banquet; it's always the richest who are toasted first.

闹市挣钱，静处安身。

Make money in the hectic city, settle down in the quiet countryside.

来如风雨，去似微尘。

We're born like wind and rain and pass away like dust and dirt.

长江后浪推前浪，世上新人换旧人。

The waves behind drive on those before, as youths excel older generations.

近水楼台先得月，向阳花木早逢春。

One first catches the rising moon at a waterfront pavilion. Flowers first meet spring facing the sun.

先到为君，后到为臣。

Come first as a king, then as a minister.

莫道君行早，更有早行人。

Never say a man travels early, because there are always even earlier ones.

莫信直中直，须防仁不仁。

A man boasting of his integrity needs close examination. A man boasting of his righteousness needs an audit.

古人不见今时月，今月曾经照古人。

The ancients never saw today's moon, but we stand in the light of the same moon they saw.

山中有直树，世上无直人。

There are many straight trees in the mountains, but no righteous people in the world.

自恨枝无叶，莫怨太阳偏。

A tree should blame itself for having no leaves, not blame the sun for inclining.

万般皆由命，半点不由人。

Everything is preordained; no one can change it.

一家之计在于和，一生之计在于勤。

Harmony is critical to family, and diligence is critical to success.

责人之心责己，恕己之心恕人。

Demand as much of yourself as you demand of others and forgive others as freely as you forgive yourself.

守口如瓶，防意如城。

Cork your mouth tight like a bottle, and guard against selfish desire like a fortification.

宁可人负我，切莫我负人。

It is better for others to wrong me than for me to wrong others.

再三须慎意，第一莫欺心。

Think twice before you act but follow your heart before justifying it.

虎生犹可近，人熟不堪亲。

You can come close to a tiger but be more cautious around people you know.

来说是非者，便是是非人。

People who gossip about others are not trustworthy.

远水难救近火，远亲不如近邻。

Faraway water won't douse a nearby fire; a good neighbor is better than a faraway brother

有茶有酒多兄弟，急难何曾见一人。

Friends are everywhere when you have wine and delicacies. No one is around when you have hardship and suffering.

人情似纸张张薄，世事如棋局局新。

Human associations are as fragile as paper sheets, and secular affairs are as unpredictable as chess games.

山中也有千年树，世上难逢百岁人。

A thousand-year tree is common, but a hundred-year man is rare.

力微休负重，言轻莫劝人。

Weak ones don't bear weights; weak words don't persuade others.

无钱休入众，遭难莫寻亲。

Don't crowd in when you are poor; don't ask relatives for help when you are in hard times.

平生不做皱眉事，世上应无切齿人。

Don't do wicked things, and no one will hate you.

士乃国之宝，儒为席上珍。

Scholars are the wealth of a country, and Confucians are the treasures at a banquet.

若要断酒法，醒眼看醉人。

If you want to quit drinking, look at drunks when you are sober.

白酒酿成缘好客，黄金散尽为诗书。

The wine is brewed for friends, and the fortune is spent on books.

渴时一滴如甘露，醉后添杯不如无。

A drop of water is like nectar to a thirsty man. A glass of wine is useless to a drunken man.

惜钱休教子，护短莫从师。

Don't spare money in educating the young, and don't be too protective when the teachers discipline your kids.

久住令人贱，频来亲也疏。

Lodging for too long makes people annoying; visiting relatives too frequently makes people distant.

酒中不语真君子，财上分明大丈夫。

Gentlemen don't rave after drink; gentleman don't obscure when keeping accounts.

贫贱之交不可忘，糟糠之妻不下堂。

Don't forget the friends you made when you were poor. Don't abandon your wife who shared your suffering.

出家如初，成佛有余。

Don't forget your humble beginnings as a monk; it is enough for you to become a buddha.

积金千两，不如明解经书。

Saving thousands of dollars is no more valuable than having a clear understanding of the sage's wisdom.

水至清则无鱼，人至察则无徒。

Clear water survives no fish. When the master is too strict, there will be no disciples.

求人须求英雄汉，济人须济急时无。

Ask a gentleman for help and help others who are in real need.

有田不耕仓廪虚，有书不读子孙愚。

The granary will be empty if the field isn't cultivated, and children will be ignorant if they don't read books.

仓廪虚兮岁月乏，子孙愚兮礼仪疏。

An empty granary doesn't guarantee a good life; ignorant offspring don't know manners.

听君一席话，胜读十年书。

Talking with a wise man for one moment is more inspiring than reading books for ten years.

养子不教如养驴，养女不教如养猪。

Raising a boy without educating him is worse than raising a donkey and raising a girl without educating her is worse than raising a pig.

人不通古今，马牛如襟裾。

A man who doesn't know history is like a beast of the field wearing a man's clothes.

茫茫四海人无数，哪个男儿是丈夫。

There are countless people in the world, but few are real heroes.

救人一命，胜造七级浮屠。

Saving one life is more benevolent than building a seven-story stupa.

城门失火，殃及池鱼。

A fire on the city gate, no fish in the city moat.

庭前生瑞草，好事不如无。

The auspicious grass grown, the green-eyed monster is attracted.

欲求生富贵，须下死工夫。

If you want to get riches and honor, you have to devote toil and moil.

百年成之不足，一旦坏之有余。

Years of hard work may not bring success, but a day of slacking can send it down the drain.

人心似铁，官法如炉。

If the human heart is like iron, the rule of law is like iron furnaces.

善化不足，恶化有余。

If education doesn't reform you, then rehabilitation will remake you.

在家由父，出嫁从夫。

A maiden must obey her father, and the wife must obey her husband.

痴人畏妇，贤女敬夫。

Only a fool is afraid of his wife, and a virtuous woman respects her husband.

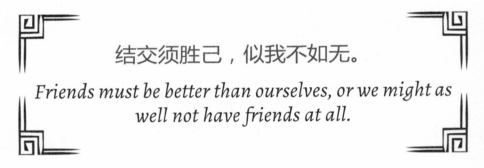

结交须胜己，似我不如无。

Friends must be better than ourselves, or we might as well not have friends at all.

知者减半，省者全无。

Smart people will only share half of their opinions, and the wise use their words very sparingly.

是非终日有，不听自然无。

There is gossip every day; if you don't listen to it, it won't exist.

竹篱茅舍风光好，道院僧房终不如。

The simple cottage has a beautiful view; even the view from the temple is not as good.

宁可正而不足，不可邪而有余。

It is better to be an upright man living in poverty than an evil man living in prosperity.

宁可信其有，不可信其无。

Better to assume the worst before it happens than to be surprised by it when it comes.

命里有时终须有，命里无时莫强求。

Something will occur if it is meant for you; otherwise, nothing will happen even if you insist.

道院迎仙客，书堂隐相儒。

The temple greets gods, the school hosts scholars.

庭栽栖凤竹，池养化龙鱼。

Bamboo planted garden is home to phoenix, and fish-feeding pond is home to dragon.

但看三五日，相见不如初。

After several days of getting along, it's no better than the first meeting.

会说说都市，不会说屋里。

Eloquent men lecture on affairs of state, but inarticulate men only gossip in the neighborhood.

人情似水分高下，世事如云任卷舒。

Feelings are as fickle as water, and life is as unpredictable as clouds.

磨刀恨不利，刀利伤人指。

The sharpening of the knife sees no end, but a sharp knife hurts fingers.

求财恨不多，财多害自己。

The pursuit of money sees no end, but a great fortune harms lives.

知足常足，终身不辱；

Enough is as good as a feast, and you won't be shamed for being greedy.

知止常止，终身不耻。

Know where to draw the line, and you will never be disgraced.

有福伤财，无福伤己。

Blessed people lose money, but unlucky people lose lives.

失之毫厘，谬以千里。

A minimal deviation may result in wide divergence.

若登高必自卑，若涉远必自迩。

Topping a high mountain makes people humble, and travelling a long distance makes people modest.

三思而行，再思可矣。

Thinking twice leads to better decisions, overthinking leads to no decisions.

使口不如亲为，求人不如求己。

It is better to do it in person than to talk about it; it is better to
work independently than to ask for help.

墙有缝，壁有耳。

There are cracks in the wall, and there are ears behind the wall.

嫉财莫嫉食，怨生莫怨死。

Envy others' wealth but not their diet; blame while others are
alive but not after their death.

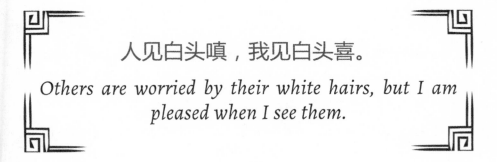

人见白头嗔，我见白头喜。

*Others are worried by their white hairs, but I am
pleased when I see them.*

多少少年郎，不到白头死。

So many young people die with black hair who have not lived
long enough to have white hair.

小时是兄弟，长大各乡里。

Playmates are close when they are kids, and drift apart when
they grow up.

好事不出门，坏事传千里。

Good deeds go unsung, while bad news is broadcast.

晴天不肯去，直待雨淋头。

If you put off going when the weather is good, you may have to go in the pouring rain.

成事莫说，覆水难收。

Don't argue a fact or try to collect spilled water.

是非只为多开口，烦恼皆因强出头。

Talking too much brings troubles, as showing too much invites problems.

忍得一时之气，免得百日之忧。

Keeping your temper in the moment avoids trouble for a long time.

近来学得乌龟法，得缩头时且缩头。

Imitate the tortoise in its shell, and pull in your head when it's prudent.

惧法朝朝乐，欺心日日忧。

Law-abiding guarantees free and happy, while law-breaking brings fear and worry.

人生一世，草长一秋。

The lifecycle of a man is as brief as a year to the grass.

月过十五光明少，人到中年万事休。

There will be less light after a full moon; there will less ambition by middle age.

儿孙自有儿孙福，莫为儿孙做马牛。

Children have their own lives to live, and parents have their
hold to release.

为人莫做千年计，三十河东四十西。

Don't plan for too long; things are too unpredictable.

人生不满百，常怀千岁忧。

A hundred-year life is rare, but a thousand years of worries
are common.

今朝有酒今朝醉，明日愁来明日忧。

Toast and be drunk today, tomorrow's sorrow will wait
until tomorrow.

路逢险处须回避，事到临头不自由。

You can avoid danger when you're walking, but you can't dodge
it when troubles are looming.

三杯通大道，一醉解千愁。

Three shots can end a thousand worries.

一家养女百家求，一马不行百马忧。

A beautiful daughter will have many suitors, while a bad lead
horse will slow many other horses.

有花方酌酒，无月不登楼。

Drink when the flowers bloom; ascend with the harvest moon.

贼是小人，智过君子。

Although thieves are villains, their wisdom can sometimes surpass the gentlemen's.

君子固穷，小人穷斯滥矣。

A gentleman in poverty restrains himself, but a penniless villain commits crimes.

不以我为德，反以我为仇。

Instead of thanking me, treat me as an enemy.

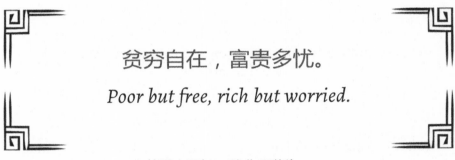

贫穷自在，富贵多忧。

Poor but free, rich but worried.

若要人不知，除非己莫为。

If you don't want people to know, you'd better not do it.

为人不做亏心事，半夜敲门心不惊。

If a man does nothing wrong, he won't panic at a midnight knock.

宁向直中取，不可曲中求。

Better to fight than ever to beg.

人无远虑，必有近忧。

A man without a long-term plan will be troubled in the near future.

休别有鱼处，莫恋浅滩头。

Don't let curiosity drive you from where the fish are biting, just to explore an unknown shoal.

去时终须去，再三留不住。

Everything leaves when it's time, and all your desire can't keep it from going.

忍一句，息一怒，饶一着，退一步。

Hold back a word and calm down a fury. If you forgive others, others will accommodate you.

三十不豪，四十不富，五十将衰寻子助。

Be self-reliant by the age of thirty and be rich by the age of forty. If not, you won't have much to look forward to at fifty.

生不认魂，死不认尸。

He who has not prepared for old age must prepare to depend on others when it comes.

一寸光阴一寸金，寸金难买寸光阴。

Time is gold, but gold is not time.

黑发不知勤学早，转眼便是白头翁。

If one doesn't study in youth, he will regret when he's old.

父母恩深终有别，夫妻义重也分离。

The parents pass away regardless of deep affection, and the couple breaks up regardless of solemn vows.

人生似鸟同林宿，大难来时各自飞。

We are birds perching in the same forest, and each will fly away when disaster strikes.

人善被人欺，马善被人骑。

Kind people are often bullied by others, and tamed horses can't choose their riders.

人无横财不富，马无夜草不肥。

People can't get rich without making an unexpected fortune, and horses can't grow fat without eating night grass.

人恶人怕天不怕，人善人欺天不欺。

People are scared of wicked people but not the God; kind people are bullied by others but not the God.

善恶到头终有报，只盼来早与来迟。

Kind or evil, karma comes in the end; the justice will be served sooner or later.

黄河尚有澄清日，岂能人无得运时。

There is a season when the Yellow River runs clear; why is there is no season for one to get lucky?

得宠思辱，居安思危。

When you are favored, prepare for the shame that you may suffer in the future. When you are safe, consider the dangers that may threaten in the future.

人贫不语，水平不流。

A man does not talk much when he is poor, and water does not
flow when terrain is gentle.

深山毕竟藏猛虎，大海终须纳细流。

The mountain inevitably hides tigers, and the sea eventually
embraces trickles.

大抵选她肌骨好，不搽红粉也风流。

A natural beauty isn't enhanced by makeup.

莫待是非来入耳，从前恩爱反为仇。

*Don't let right or wrong come into your ears,
turning love into bitterness.*

惜花须检点，爱月不梳头。

A sensitive man never fools around, and a pure lady never
degrades herself.

受恩深处宜先退，得意浓时便可休。

It's wise to retreat when in the depths of grace, and to stop in
time when riding on the crest of success.

留得五湖明月在，不愁无处下金钩。

As long as the lake is there, one always catches fish in the future.

念念有如临敌日，心心常似过桥时。

Be as vigilant as if you were facing an enemy and be as cautious as if you were crossing a bridge.

英雄行险道，富贵似花枝。

The road taken by a hero is full of hardships, and glory and wealth wither as certainly as flowers.

人情莫道春光好，只怕秋来有冷时。

Human relations are not always as warm as a spring breeze; there may be times when it is as cold and clear as autumn.

送君千里，终有一别。

As much as you don't want to see your friends leaving, you still have to say good-bye.

但将冷眼观螃蟹，看你横行到几时。

Look at the crawling crab with a calm eye and see how long it can dominate.

见事莫说，问事不知。

Don't say a word when you see something; say you don't know when others ask.

善事可做，恶事莫为。

Do good deeds; never do bad deeds.

假缎染就真红色，也被旁人说是非。

Dye the fake satin red, but gossip will still arise.

闲事莫管，无事早归。

Don't mind other people's business; go home when your own
is done.

许人一物，千金不移。

A promise is worth a thousand pieces of gold.

龙生龙子，虎生虎儿。

Dragons beget dragons, tigers beget tigers.

龙游浅水遭虾戏，虎落平阳被犬欺。

The shrimp dared to tease a dragon in shallow water; the dogs
dared to bully a tiger on the wild plains.

一举首登龙虎榜，十年身到凤凰池。

Get first place in your first try at the imperial examination, and
you can make ambitious plans after ten years of hard work.

十年寒窗无人问，一举成名天下知。

No one knows about ten years of hard work, but everyone
knows who got first place.

酒债寻常处处有，人生七十古来稀。

Drinking debt is common, but an octogenarian is rare.

养儿防老，积谷防饥。

Raising children prepares for when one is old as storing grain
prepares for when there is a famine.

鸡豚狗彘之畜，无失其时，数口之家，可以无饥矣。

If livestock don't miss their time of breeding, families will not suffer from famine.

道吾好者是吾贼，道吾恶者是吾师。

People who flatter me are hurting me, but people who criticize me are helping me.

好言难得，恶语易施。

It's hard to get praise but easy to point fingers.

入门休问荣枯事，且看容颜便得知。

Don't ask the host how everything's going, just look at his face and you will know.

当家才知盐米贵，养子方知父母恩。

Only when you keep a house can you realize that money is hard to earn, and only when you become parent can you understand the grace from parents.

常将有日思无日，莫把无时当有时。

When life is good, always think about the times when you were poor, and don't be as extravagant and wasteful as you were when you were rich.

树欲静而风不止，子欲养而亲不待。

The tree wants to stand still, but the wind keeps blowing.

When the son hopes to be filial to his parents, his parents have already died.

时来风送滕王阁，运去雷轰荐福碑。

When you are lucky, even bad situations can be met with good luck. When you are unlucky, the good situation will turn bad.

官清司吏瘦，神灵庙祝肥。

In honest and incorrupt governments, officials are not rich; efficacious gods enrich the temple.

息却雷霆之怒，罢却虎豹之威。

Calm the thunder of your anger and quit threatening like a tiger.

饶人算之本，输人算之机。

Forgiveness is the basis of long-term winning, and short-term compromise is the key to long-term winning.

一言既出，驷马难追。

One should keep a promise and let nothing change it.

路逢侠客须呈剑，不是才人莫献诗。

Gift the knight a sword; and don't write poetry for the illiterate.

三人同行，必有我师。择其善者而从之，其不善者而改之。

When three people are together, one could be your teacher. Follow the good and correct the bad.

欲昌和顺须为善，要振家声在读书。

Do good for family harmony; Study hard to revitalize the family.

少壮不努力，老大徒伤悲。

When I was young, I didn't study hard. When I was old, I didn't achieve anything.

人有善愿，天必佑之。

People have good wishes, and God will bless them.

莫饮卯时酒，昏昏醉到酉。

Drink alcohol in the morning, and you'll waste your day in happy intoxication.

莫骂酉时妻，一夜受孤凄。

Don't quarrel with your wife at night, or you will be lonely all night.

种麻得麻，种豆得豆。

Plant hemp and get hemp, plant beans and get beans.

百世修来同船渡，千世修来共枕眠。

Hundreds of reincarnations come from sharing the same boat; thousands of reincarnations come from sharing the same bed.

见官莫向前，作客莫在后。

Don't show off when meeting officials, and don't back down when visiting friends.

宁添一斗，莫添一口。

One would add another bucket of food, rather than add one more person in the family.

螳螂捕蝉，岂知黄雀在后。

When the praying mantis caught the cicada, he didn't expect the carduelis to be behind it.

天网恢恢，疏而不漏。

Sooner or later, justice will be served.

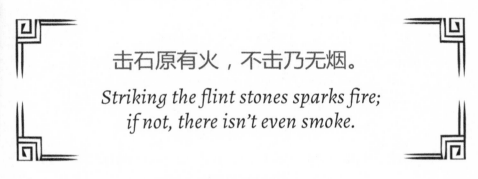

击石原有火，不击乃无烟。

*Striking the flint stones sparks fire;
if not, there isn't even smoke.*

不求金玉重重贵，但愿儿孙个个贤。

Do not chase gold or jade, only hope the future generations are promising.

一日夫妻，百世姻缘。

Marriage for one day comes from the karma of hundreds of reincarnations.

杀人一万，自损三千。

When you hurt others, you will also suffer.

伤人一语，利如刀割。

Saying something that hurts another is like cutting someone's heart with a knife.

枯木逢春犹再发，人无两度再少年。

Withered trees can germinate again in spring, but we will not have the chance to be young again.

未晚先投宿，鸡鸣早看天。

Find a lodging before dusk. Hit the road before dawn.

将相顶头堪走马，公侯肚内好撑船。

A general's mind is wide enough for riding a horse. A prime minister's mind is broad enough for poling a boat.

富人思来年，穷人想眼前。

The rich prepare for the future, but the poor only consider the moment.

世上若要人情好，赊去物品莫取钱。

If you want to gain popularity, don't charge others what they owe you.

生死有命，富贵在天。

Life and death are destined, and wealth is arranged by God.

莫笑他人老，终须还到老。

Don't joke about others getting old; you will get old eventually.

人学始知道，不学亦徒然。

Only when people learn will they understand the truth, and if they don't learn, they will know nothing.

和得邻里好，犹如拾片宝。

Getting along with the neighborhood is as valuable as picking up treasures.

但能守本分，终身无烦恼。

As long as we live in peace, we will have no troubles in our lives.

大家做事寻常，小家做事慌张。

Big and rich households handle things calmly, but small and poor households tend to panic in many situations.

大家礼义教子弟，小家凶恶训儿郎。

Big and rich households teach their children with politeness, while small and poor households only reprimand their children with bad words.

君子爱财，取之有道。

Gentlemen love money, but they obtain it from proper channels.

贞妇爱色，纳之以礼。

Ladies like to dress up, but they meet the rules of etiquette.

善有善报，恶有恶报。

Good is returned for good deeds, as bad is the retribution for bad deeds.

家中不和邻里欺，邻里不和说是非。

An unharmonious family is bullied by the neighbors. An unfriendly neighborhood invokes spats.

万恶淫为首，百善孝当先。

Adultery led all sins, and filial piety led all virtues.

人而无信，不知其可也。

If one fails to keep a promise, I really don't know what else he can do.

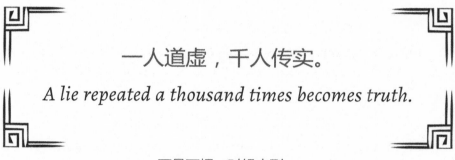

一人道虚，千人传实。

A lie repeated a thousand times becomes truth.

不是不报，时候未到。

Retribution comes when it's time.

凡事要好，须问三老。

Ask three respected elders before acting.

若争小利，便失大道。

To haggle over petty gains harms bigger morals.

年年防饥，夜夜防盗。

Beware of famine every year and beware of thieves every night.

学者是好，不学不好。

An intellectual likes to read, but an illiterate is always
disgusted by it.

学者如禾如稻，不学如草如蒿。

An intellectual is as useful as grain, while an ignorant person is
as useless as grass.

遇饮酒时须防醉，得高歌处且高歌。

Whenever you have a chance to drink, be careful not to be drunk.
Whenever you have a chance to sing, let go of your throat.

因风吹火，用力不多。

Use the wind to blow the fire and save your breath.

不因渔夫引，怎能见波涛。

Without the guidance of the fisherman, one can never see
the waves.

无求到处人情好，不饮任他酒价高。

If you don't beg for help, your relationships with others will be
good. If you don't drink, you will not care for the price.

知事少时烦恼少，识人多处是非多。

The less you know, the less worry you will have. The more people
you know, the more trouble will accompany them.

进山不怕伤人虎，只怕人情两面刀。

I am not afraid of tigers, but I fear those two-faced villains.

世间好语书说尽，天下名山僧占多。

Good things have been exhausted by books, and famous
mountains have been occupied by monks.

强中更有强中手，恶人须用恶人磨。

There will be stronger people among the strong, and the wicked
will eventually be subdued by the worse.

会使不在家富豪，风流不用衣着多。

Talents do not derive from the wealth of the family, and
elegance does not derive from wearing gorgeous clothes.

光阴似箭，日月如梭。

Time flies like arrows, sun and moon like shuttles.

天时不如地利，地利不如人和。

Timing is not as critical as favorable terrain, and favorable
terrain is not as critical as unity of people.

黄金未为贵，安乐值钱多。

Gold is not the most valuable thing—peace is.

为善最乐，作恶难逃。

Doing good is the most enjoyable; doing evil is hard to escape.

羊有跪乳之恩，鸦有反哺之情。

Sheep have the grace of kneeling and breastfeeding, and the
crows have the feeling of feeding back their elders.

孝顺还生孝顺子，忤逆还生忤逆儿。

Filial men beget filial sons, disobedient men raise disobedient sons.

不信但看檐前水，点点滴滴旧池窝。

Just like the water in front of the eaves, bit by bit drips into the old pool.

隐恶扬善，执其两端。

Restrain evil and promote good and hold on to both approaches.

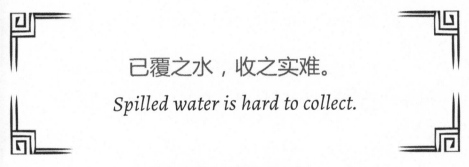

已覆之水，收之实难。

Spilled water is hard to collect.

妻贤夫祸少，子孝父心宽。

A husband has few troubles with a virtuous wife; the father is at ease with a filial son.

人生知足时常足，人老偷闲且是闲。

Life is satisfying if one is content; leisure and comfort lie in the elderly times.

用心计较般般错，退后思量事事宽。

Closed-minded brings troubles and worries; open-minded brings ease and comfort.

处处绿杨堪系马，家家有路通长安。
Every tree can tie a horse, every road leads to Rome.

既坠釜甑，反顾无益。
Looking back at a smashed kettle will not mend it.

见者易，学者难。
It's easier said than done.

莫将容易得，便作等闲看。
Don't take things coming easily for granted.

厌静还思喧，嫌喧又忆山。
Missing bustle in tranquility; missing tranquility in bustle.

自从心定后，无处不安然。
Since my mind was settled, there was no restlessness.

道路各别，养家一般。
The paths may be different, but the principles of life are the same.

由俭入奢易，从奢入俭难。
It is easy to change from frugality to luxury, but difficult to
change from luxury to frugality.

知音说与知音听，不是知音莫与谈。
It's easy to talk with people who share your values.

点石化为金，人心犹未足。

Turning rocks into gold cannot satisfy a greedy man.

信了赌，卖了屋。

Gambling blinds a man to sell the house.

他人观花，不涉你目。

Others look at flowers without obstructing your eyes.

他人碌碌，不涉你足。

Others are busy without affecting your walking.

谁人不爱子孙贤，谁人不爱千钟粟。

Everyone wants the promise of offspring; everyone wants a
wealthy family.

奈五行，不是这般题目。

But the five elements of "benevolence, righteousness, courtesy,
wisdom, and faith" do not include these.

莫把真心空计较，儿孙自有儿孙福。

Don't worry about the future of your children for they have their
own blessings.

书到用时方恨少，事非经过不知难。

It is when you are applying what you have learned from
books that you wish you had read more books than you have;
it is when you have personally experienced a thing that you
understand the difficulties not known before.

天下无不是的父母，世上最难得者兄弟。

Parents are always right; brothers are the most precious.

无钱方断酒，临老始读经。

Give up drinking when there is no money; read the classics
when in the dying year.

路不铲不平，事不为不成。

The road will not be smooth if it is not shoveled, and things will
not succeed if they are not done.

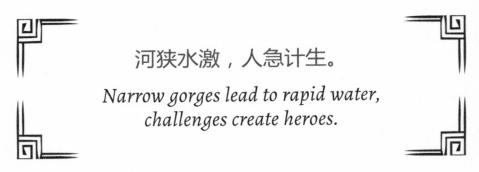

河狭水激，人急计生。

*Narrow gorges lead to rapid water,
challenges create heroes.*

不交僧道，便是好人。

A successful man doesn't associate with monks and Taoists.

但行好事，莫问前程。

Do good deeds without asking for reward.

与人不和，劝人养鹅；与人不睦，劝人架屋。

If you have problems with friends, persuade them to raise
geese. Geese can lay eggs, provide meat and can guard a house
like dogs; if you have problems with neighbors, persuade them
to build a house. Building a house tends to get all neighbors
together to help.

明知山有虎，莫向虎山行。

Don't go to the mountains where you know there are tigers.

点塔七层，不如暗处一灯。

A single candle in the darkness can be more valuable than a brightly lit seven-story pagoda.

堂上二老是活佛，何用灵山朝世尊。

The two elderly parents in the family are living Buddhas, so why go to Lingshan to worship the Buddha?

万事劝人休瞒昧，举头三尺有神明。

Don't conceal evil deeds for there are gods watching nearby.

但存方寸土，留与子孙耕。

Just save a piece of field, leave it to children to cultivate.

灭却心头火，剔起佛前灯。

Extinguish the lust in the heart, brighten the light in front of the Buddha.

惺惺多不足，蒙蒙作公卿。

The clever don't get the opportunity to display their talents, but the stupid often serve as high officials.

众星朗朗，不如孤月独明。

The shining stars are not as bright as the moon.

兄弟相害，不如友生。

It is better to have friends helping each other than brothers hurting each other.

合理可作，小利不争。

Do what is reasonable and don't fuss about petty profits.

牡丹花好空入目，枣花虽小结实多。

The peony flowers are gorgeous but only for people to admire; the jujube flowers are small but bear fruits.

欺老莫欺小，欺人心不明。

Don't bully the young since they will seek revenge when they grow up, and a bullying man is stupid.

勤奋耕锄收地利，他时饱暖谢苍天。

Plant and harvest crops according to the farming time. Don't forget to thank God when you are full and warm.

得忍且忍，得耐且耐，不忍不耐，小事成灾。

If you can bear it, bear it. If not, small troubles lead to big disasters.

相论逞英豪，家计渐渐退。

During meetings with others, if you just want to brag about your wealth, your family fortune will inevitably gradually deteriorate.

色即是空，空即是色。

Everything is changing.

一人有庆，兆民咸赖。

One person in power has something worth celebrating, and hundreds of millions of people will benefit from it.

人老心未老，人穷志莫穷。

An old man should have young mind; a poor man should have ambition.

黄蜂一口针，橘子两边分。

The wasp's needle can split an orange in half.

屋漏更遭连夜雨，行船又遇打头风。

A leaky roof meets heavy rain; a sailing ship meets oncoming wind.

人无千日好，花无百日红。

Life cannot go smoothly forever; flowers cannot bloom vigorously forever.

世间痛恨事，最毒淫妇心。

A man's viciousness can destroy everything.

杀人可恕，情理不容。

A crime can be pardoned by law, but it cannot be tolerated against humanity.

乍富不知新受用，乍贫难改旧家风。

From poor to rich, one never knows how to enjoy; from rich to poor, one never knows how to save.

贤妇令夫贵，恶妇令夫败。

A virtuous wife can help her husband succeed, and a wicked wife can make her husband fail.

座上客常满，杯中酒不空。

The banquet is often full of guests, and the glass is often full of wine.

笋因落箨方成竹，鱼为奔波始化龙。

Bamboo shoots grow tall due to the peeling off of their husks, while fishes turn into dragons due to pushing against the waves.

记得少年骑竹马，转眼又是白头翁。

I still remember riding a bamboo horse when I was young, and in a blink of an eye I became a gray-haired old man.

礼义生于富足，盗贼出于赌博。

Rites and justice are formed from a rich life, and thieves often commit crimes because of gambling.

有缘千里来相会，无缘对面不相逢。

If they are destined for each other, they can meet even if they are thousands of miles apart; if not, they will not meet each other even though they collide.

天上众星皆拱北，世间无水不朝东。

The stars in the sky are all facing the Big Dipper, and the rivers on the ground are all flowing eastward.

士为知己者死，女为悦己者容。

Men are willing to die for those who appreciate and understand them, women are willing to dress up for those who appreciate and adore them.

君子安贫，达人知命。

A noble gentleman is content in poverty; a reasonable man understands the destiny.

良药苦口利于病，忠言逆耳利于行。

Drugs taste bitter but are good for health, while criticism sounds harsh but is good for life.

顺天者昌，逆天者亡。

Only those who obey the providence thrive, and those who violate the providence perish.

有福者昌，无福者亡。

Those who are blessed prosper and thrive; those who are not blessed decay and perish.

红粉易妆娇态女，无钱难作好儿郎。

A girl can be a beauty with next to no makeup, but a man cannot be a hero without money.

人为财死，鸟为食亡。

People die for money; birds die for food.

富贵定要依本分，贫穷不必枉思量。

A rich man should keep his duty; a poor man should not worry too much.

有子之人贫不久，无儿无女富不长。

Those who have sons will not be poor forever, and those who have no children will not be rich forever.

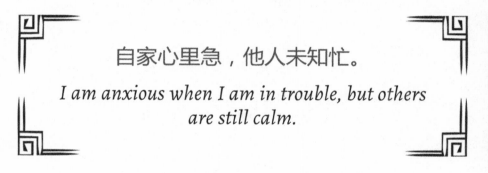

自家心里急，他人未知忙。

I am anxious when I am in trouble, but others are still calm.

夫妻相和好，琴瑟与笙簧。

Husband and wife who live in harmony are like a symphony.

善必寿老，恶必早亡。

Good people must live long, wicked people will die early.

爽口食多偏作病，快心事过恐遭殃。

Gluttonous gets you sick; triumphant gets you trouble.

贪他一斗米，失却半年粮。

Greedy to grab a bucket of rice but lose the food for half a year.

画水无风空作浪，绣花虽好不闻香。

The waves on the painting rise without wind, the flowers on the embroidery bloom without fragrance.

争他一脚豚，反失一肘羊。

Compete for a trotter but lose half of a sheep.

龙归晚洞云犹湿，麝过春山草木香。

When the dragon returns to the cave at night, the clouds are still wet; the musk jumps over the spring mountains, and the vegetation is fragrant.

平生只会说人短，何不回头把己量。

Don't discuss the shortcomings of others; why not review your own faults?

见善如不及，见恶如探汤。

Learn from good people and avoid bad people as you'd avoid boiling water.

人穷志短，马瘦毛长。

A poor man has insufficient ambition; a thin horse has long hair.

贫无达士将金赠，病有高人说药方。

There is no good-hearted man to give money when in poverty; there are able people to tell the prescription when in sickness.

万事前身定，浮生空自忙。

Everything is destined, but people are busy all their lives.

触来莫与竞，事过心清凉。

Don't compete with him if someone offends you; you will feel relieved when the matter is over.

秋来满山多秀色，春来无处不花香。

The mountains are beautiful in autumn, and the fragrance of flowers is everywhere in spring.

凡人不可貌相，海水不可斗量。

A man cannot be judged by his appearance alone, and the sea cannot be measured by a bucket.

清清之水为土所防，济济之士为酒所伤。

The clear water was blocked by the earth embankment, and many talents were injured by overdrinking.

蒿草之下或有兰香，茅茨之屋或有侯王。

There may be fragrant orchids under the wormwood, and there may be a prince in the hut.

无限朱门生饿殍，几多白屋出公卿。

Many wealthy families later on starve to death, many poor families raise senior officials.

拂石坐来春衫冷，踏花归去马蹄香。

Coldness of early spring penetrated the clothes when sitting on a rock; fragrance of flowers left on the horse's hooves when riding it back home.

酒里乾坤大，壶中日月长。

When I get drunk, I feel that the world is bigger than usual, and the time is longer than usual.

叫月子规喉舌冷，宿花蝴蝶梦魂香。

The tongue of the cuckoo bird calling at the moon is cold, and the butterfly living on the flower dreams very fragrantly.

一人传虚，百人传实。

One person tells the lie, a hundred people tell the truth.

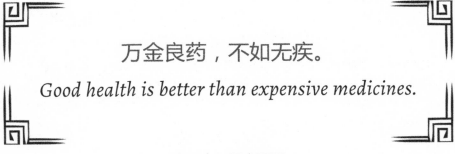

万金良药，不如无疾。

Good health is better than expensive medicines.

一言不中，千言不用。

If one word does not make the point, others are useless.

千里送鹅毛，礼轻情义重。

Send a single fine hair from a thousand miles away; the gift is light but heavy in meaning.

人生一世，如驹过隙。

Life passes as fast as a horse jumping over a crevasse.

君子怀刑，小人怀惠。

The gentleman thinks of morals, while the villain thinks of benefits.

世事如明镜，前程暗似漆。

Everything is as clear as a mirror, but the future is as dark as at night.

架上碗儿轮流转，媳妇自有做婆时。

The rice bowls in the cupboard will be replaced in their turn; today's daughter-in-law will be the mother-in-law someday.

良田万顷，日食一升。

Have one thousand acres of fertile fields but only eat one liter of rice a day.

大厦千间，夜眠八尺。

Have one thousand rooms in a castle but only sleep at an eight-foot-long bed every night.

千经万典，孝义为先。

There are thousands of classic truths; filial piety is the first and foremost.

天上人间，方便第一

No matter where you go, offer courtesy and precedence to others.

一字入公门，九牛拔不出。

The paper was sent to the government, and I was tired of litigation.

八字衙门向南开，有理无钱莫进来。

The government office door is wide open, but do not come in if you have good cause but no money.

欲求天下事，须用世间财。

Wealth brings everything.

富从升合起，贫因不算来。

Wealth comes from planning, while poverty comes from lack of it.

近河不得枉使水，近山不得枉烧柴。

Don't waste water though near the river; don't waste firewood though near the mountains.

家无读书子，官从何处来。

If the children in the family do not study, they have no chance of becoming high-ranking officials.

慈不掌兵，义不掌财。

A soft-hearted man is not suited for leading an army. A generous man is not suited for managing money.

一夫当关，万夫莫开。

One person controls the pass, thousands of people cannot get in.

万事不由人计较，一生都是命安排。

There is no need to compete with others for life is destined by fate.

白云本是无心物，却被清风引出来。

Cloud was originally an unintentional object but was drawn out by the breeze.

慢行急行，逆取顺取。

Do things slowly or urgently, your lifetime is the same; acquire wealth in this way or that way, the amount is the same.

命中只有如许财，丝毫不可有闪失。

There is only a limited amount of money in life, so take care of every penny.

人间私语，天闻若雷。

Private conversations in the world sound like thunder to God.

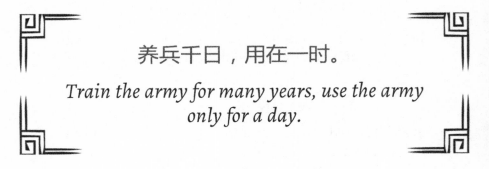

养兵千日，用在一时。

Train the army for many years, use the army only for a day.

暗室亏心，神目如电。

When doing bad things in the dark room, God can see you as clearly as if the lights were on.

一毫之恶，劝人莫作。一毫之善，与人方便。

Don't do even the smallest number of bad deeds; go for the smallest number of good deeds.

亏人是祸，饶人是福，天眼恢恢，报应甚速。

Deceiving others brings disaster sooner or later; forgiving others brings luck sooner or later; God's eyes are very bright, and retribution comes very fast.

圣贤言语，神钦鬼服。

Gods and ghosts admire what the saints say.

人各有心，心各有见。

Everyone has his own mind, and every man has his own opinion.

口说不如身逢，耳闻不如目见。

It's better to see and experience in person rather than hearing from others.

见人富贵生欢喜，莫把心头似火烧。

Don't be jealous when you see people rich and comfortable.

国清才子贵，家富小儿娇。

National politics are incorrupt and talented people are respected, and children are spoiled when their families are rich.

利刀割体疮犹使，恶语伤人恨不消。

The sharp sword cuts through the skin and the wound will heal but the vicious words hurt the heart and the wound will not disappear.

公道世间唯白发，贵人头上不曾饶。

The fairest thing in the world is old age; white hair comes to the rich and the poor alike.

为官须作相，及第必争先。

An official should work hard to be the prime minister, and the imperial examination candidates must compete for the first place.

有才堪出众，无衣懒出门。

Talents brings success; laziness won't even bring you outdoors.

苗从地发，树由枝分。

The seedlings germinate from the ground, and the big tree grows from the branches.

宅里燃火，烟气成云。

The smoke becomes a cloud when a fire is burnt in the home.

以直报怨，知恩报恩。

Repay grievances with grace; repay kindness with gratitude.

红颜今日虽欺我，白发他时不放君。

Although you can use your youth to deceive me today, it won't be long before white hairs will come to you as well.

借问酒家何处有，牧童遥指杏花村。

If you ask where there are restaurants, the shepherd boy points to Xinghua Village.

父子和而家不退，兄弟和而家不分。

The family will not decline when father and son are in unity; the family will not split when brothers are in harmony.

一片云间不相识，三千里外却逢君。

One may not know another under the same cloud, but we are friends even three thousand miles apart.

官有公法，民有私约。

The government has national laws, and the people have private contracts.

平时不烧香，临时抱佛脚。

Never burn incense and worship Buddha in spare time but embrace the Buddha's feet and ask for help in a crisis.

争得猫儿，失却牛脚。

Snatched the cat but lost the cow.

惜花春起早，爱月夜眠迟。

Cherish the flower and get up early; love the moon and sleep late.

幸生太平无事日，恐防年老不多时。

Fortunate to be born in peaceful years, I'm afraid that the days are passing by.

国乱思良将，家贫思良妻。

A chaotic country is in desperate need of capable generals; a poor family is in desperate need of a virtuous wife.

池塘积水须防旱，田地深耕足养家。

Water should be stored in the pond to safeguard against drought, and the field should be cultivated carefully to feed the family.

根深不怕风摇动，树正何愁月影斜。

Trees with deep roots are not afraid of violent winds; trunks
that grow straight are not afraid of the moon shadow's slanting.

愚者千虑，必有一得，智者千虑，必有一失。

The fool has a thousand worries and must have a gain, and the
wise one has a thousand worries and must have a loss.

始吾于人也，听其言而信其行。

Once, behavior is trusted after hearing what he said.

今吾于人也，听其言而观其行。

Now, behavior is still observed after hearing what he said.

哪个梳头无乱发，情人眼里出西施。

Even with messy hair, the lover's eyes see only beauty.

珠沉渊而川媚，玉韫石而山辉。

The pearl laying in the riverbed makes the water shimmer, and
the jade contained in the rocks makes the mountains shine.

夕阳无限好，只恐不多时。

The glow of the sunset is magnificent, but it will not last long.

久旱逢甘霖，他乡遇故知

Meeting an old friend far away from home is like a long drought
meeting the refreshing rain.

洞房花烛夜，金榜题名时。

Enjoying the wedding night in bridal chamber, topping the national exam with excellent scores.

掬水月在手，弄花香满衣。

Holding up the moon shone in the mountain spring, fiddling with the flowers and the fragrance permeates the clothes.

桃红李白蔷薇紫，问着东君总不知。

The gorgeous color of the blossom is beautiful, but the god of Spring isn't aware.

教子教孙须教义，栽桑栽柘少栽花。

Educate children to be virtuous. Cultivate farmland rather than raising flowers.

休念故乡生处好，受恩深处便为家。

No need to miss our birthplace, home is where we are most deeply favored by others.

学在一人之下，用在万人之上。

Learn from one teacher and apply to thousands of people.

一日为师，终生为父。

A teacher for a day is a father for life.

忘恩负义，禽兽之徒。

An ungrateful person is less than a beast.

劝君莫将油炒菜，留与儿孙夜读书。

Leave the oil for children to read by at night, rather than cooking.

书中自有千钟粟，书中自有颜如玉。

There are a thousand buckets of millet in books, and there is beautiful jade in books.

作善鬼神钦，作恶遭天遣。

Ghosts will admire good deeds, and evil deeds will be punished by gods.

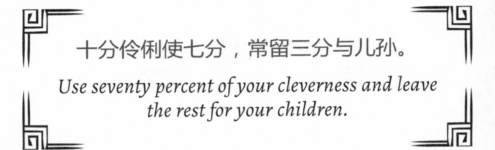

十分伶俐使七分，常留三分与儿孙。

Use seventy percent of your cleverness and leave the rest for your children.

若要十分都使尽，远在儿孙近在身。

If you don't, your children may suffer in consequence.

莫怨天来莫怨人，五行八字命生成。

Don't complain, everything is destined.

莫怨自己穷，穷要穷得干净。

Don't complain that you are poor, be poor and be decent.

莫羡他人富，富要富得清高。

Don't envy mere wealth; strive to be both rich and be noble.

别人骑马我骑驴，仔细思量我不如。

I ride a donkey while others ride horseback, thus must I be
inferior to them?

待我回头看，还有挑脚汉。

But when I look around, there are people far less fortunate than I.

路上有饥人，家中有剩饭。

Hungry people on the road and leftovers at home.

积德与儿孙，要广行方便。

Accumulate virtue for the children, provide a meal for the hungry.

积钱积谷不如积德，买田买地不如买书。

Acquiring money and food is not as good as acquiring morals,
and buying land and house is not as good as buying books.

一日春工十日粮，十日春工半年粮。

Work one day in spring and earn ten days' living; work ten days
in spring and earn half a year's living.

疏懒人没吃，勤俭粮满仓。

The lazy starve to death, while the thrifty live in abundance.

责人之心责己，爱己之心爱人。

Blame yourself as you blame others, and love others as you
love yourself.

好学者则庶民之子为公卿，不好学者则公卿之子为庶民。

A farmer's son can be a king if he studies hard, while a king's son can be a beggar if he idles around.

人亲财不亲，财利要分清。

Short accounts make long friends.

君子乐得做君子，小人枉自做小人。

A gentleman is happy to be a gentleman while a villain is a villain in vain.

人在家中坐，祸从天上落。

When a man sits at home, disasters fall from the heavens.

但求心无愧，不怕有后灾。

A clear conscience ensures no worries.

只有和气去迎人，哪有相打得太平。

You should only treat others with kindness. How can there be peace in fighting each other?

忠厚自有忠厚报，豪强一定受官刑。

The loyal will surely get retribution while the overbearing will surely be punished by law.

人到公门正好修，留些阴德在后头。

Practice cultivation when working in the government and leave some virtue for future planning.

记得旧文章，便是新举人。

Remember all the old articles, and you can be the new top scholar.

为人何必争高下，一旦无命万事休。

No need to compete for superiority, for everything is meaningless when you're dead.

白水变酒卖，还嫌猪无糟。

Sold the water as wine, then complained about not having lees to feed the pigs.

山高不算高，人心比天高。

The mountain is not the highest, for the human heart is higher than the sky.

贫寒休要怨，宝贵不须骄。

Don't blame others for being poor and shabby, and don't be proud and complacent about being rich.

善恶随人作，祸福自己招。

Good and evil are done by ourselves; misfortune and luck are brought on by ourselves.

善为至宝深深用，心作良田世世耕。

Goodness is the most precious treasure, enriching generation after generation.

奉劝君子，各宜守己。

Gentlemen should do everything peaceably.

只此呈示，万无一失

If you do, you're sure to be safe and sound.

前人俗语，言浅理深。

The ancient proverbs are simple but profound.

补遗增广，集成书文。

Expand the collection and integrate to a book.

世上无难事，只怕不专心。

Where there is a will, there is a way.

成人不自在，自在不成人。

Work hard to be successful, living at ease leads to failure.

金凭火炼方知色，与人交财便知心。

Gold is tested with fire while man is tested with money.

乞丐无粮，懒惰而成。

Beggars are beggars because of laziness.

勤俭为无价之宝，节粮乃众妙之门。

Diligence and thriftiness are invaluable.

省事俭用，免得求人。

Live frugally, and you won't have to trouble others.

量大祸不在，机深祸亦深。

Magnanimity turns dangers into peace; schemes lead to
endless troubles.

群居防口，独坐防心。

Avoid gossiping when in a group; avoid wild thoughts when alone.

体无病为富贵，身平安莫怨贫。

Consider yourself rich when you are free from illness, don't
complain of poverty when you enjoy good health.

败家子弟挥金如土，贫家子弟积土成金。

Prodigal children spend money like dirt, while poor children
accumulate money into gold.

富贵非关天地，祸福不是鬼神。

Wealth and poverty are not destined by God, misfortune and
happiness are not controlled by ghosts.

安分贫一时，本分终不贫。

People who follow the rules and struggle may be poor for a
while but will never be poor forever.

人过留名，雁过留声。

Reputation is as memorable as the cries of geese going overhead.

事从根起，藕叶连心。

Things start from the root, and the lotus roots connect the heart.

不拜父母拜干亲，弟兄不和结外人。

Don't disrespect your parents while respecting others' parents, don't fight with your brothers while trying to ally with others.

择子莫择父，择亲莫择邻。

You can change and mold a son but not a father, and you can change and mold a relative but not a neighbor.

不说自己井绳短，反说他人箍井深。

Don't blame oneself for bringing a short rope but complain about a deep well.

爱妻之心是主，爱子之心是亲。

The love for the wife is a kind of love from the master, while the love for the children is more affectionate.

祸与福同门，利与害同城。

Misfortune and luck are interdependent, benefit and harm are interdependent.

清酒红人脸，财帛动人心！

Wine makes a red face, and wealth makes a greedy heart!

宁可荤口念佛，不可素口骂人。

It's better to pray to the Buddha with a carnivore's mouth than to curse with a vegetarian's mouth.

有钱能说话，无钱话不灵。

Money can talk.

岂能尽如人意。但求不愧吾心。

How can it all be as desired? But please be worthy of my heart.

恩爱多生病，无钱便觉贫。

Loving couples care for each other for even minor ailments. Illness makes you feel poorer when you don't have money.

只学斟酒意，莫学下棋心。

Be generous, as when urging a drink, and don't be as competitive as when playing chess.

孝莫假意，转眼便为人父母。

Don't pretend to be filial to parents; you will be a parent in a blink.

善休望报，回头只看汝儿孙！

Good deeds don't have to ask for rewards, they will show up in children.

口开神气散，舌出是非生！

Careless talk leads to trouble.

弹琴费指甲，说话费精神。

Playing the piano costs nails, speaking costs energy.

千贯买田，万贯结邻。

Spend a thousand to buy land is not as good as spend ten thousand to form good neighbors.

人言未必犹尽，听话只听三分。

Other's words may not be completely correct, so it is best not to blindly believe them.

隔壁岂无耳，窗外岂无人。

Is there no ear next door, is there no one outside the window?

财可养生须注意，事不关己不劳心。

If you have money, you should be restrained; if something is none of your business, leave it aside.

酒不护贤，色不护病。

Drinking does not protect the virtuous, and prurience does not protect the diseased.

财不护亲，气不护命！

Money does not protect relatives; anger does not protect health!

一日不可无常业，安闲便易起邪心。

A man cannot do without a proper career even for a day. Idling around leads to evil deeds.

人情送匹马，买卖不饶针。

If it is for favors, there is no problem sending horses. But if you do business, you have to count every penny.

嫉妒人心，骨肉更甚于外人。

Jealousy is more damaging among brothers than among strangers.

瓜熟蒂落，水到渠成。

The melon will fall off when ripe; the river will form when water flows.

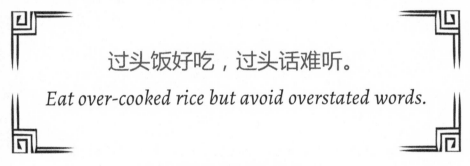

过头饭好吃，过头话难听。

Eat over-cooked rice but avoid overstated words.

炎凉世态，富贵更甚于贫贱。

Fickleness is more evident in the rich than in the poor.

事多累了自己，田多养了众人。

Too much trouble makes one tired, but too many fields feed everyone.

平心静心不欺心何等放心。

Be calm, be peaceful, be honest and you will be free from worries.

一朝权在手，便把令来行。

Once in power, give orders.

天子至尊不过于理，在理良心天下通行。

The emperors are noble simply because they know how to reason; and calm people with ethics and values are not afraid of going anywhere.

好话不在多说，有理不在高声！

Good words don't come in lengthy, reasonable words don't come in shouting!

甘草味甜人可食，巧言妄语不可听。

Licorice is sweet and wholesome; a lie sounds sweet but is poisonous.

当场不论，过后枉然。

Make it clear on the spot or else it will be useless later on.

贫莫与富斗，富莫与官争！

The poor don't fight against the rich, the rich don't fight against the officials!

官清难逃猾吏手，衙门少有念佛人。

An uncorrupted official will be framed by a cunning beadle. There are few benevolent people in the government.

家有千口，主事一人。

Only one person can run a large family.

父子竭力山成玉，弟兄同心土变金。

Concerted efforts of father and son turn mountains into jade, concerted efforts of brothers turn soil into gold.

当事者迷，旁观者清。

Those involved are confused while the bystanders are clear.

怪人不知理，知理不怪人。

It is not polite to point fingers at someone and the educated will not blame others.

未富先富终不富，未贫先贫终不贫。

Poor people who live in a rich way will not become rich. Rich people who live in a thrifty way will never be poor.

少当少取，少输当赢！

Reducing losses is gaining, narrowing the gap is winning!

饱暖思淫欲，饥寒起盗心。

Wealth brings indulgence and poverty brings theft.

蚊虫遭扇打，只因嘴伤人！

Mosquitoes were slapped, just because they hurt people with their mouths!

欲多伤神，财多累心！

Too many desires hurt your spirit and too much money makes you worry.

家贫出孝子，国乱显忠臣！

A poor family raises a filial son, and a country in chaos distinguishes a loyal minister.

布衣得暖真为福，千金平安即是春。

The common people think that as long as they live in abundance, they are truly happy; the word "peace" is worth a thousand dollars. As long as the family is safe, there is hope in life.

宁做太平犬，莫做离乱人！

I would rather be a dog in peace than a man in war!

人有几等，官有几品。

People have grades like officials have grades.

读未见书如逢良友，见已读书如逢故人。

Reading new books is like meeting new friends; re-reading good books is like meeting old friends.

理不卫亲，法不为民。

The formulation, implementation, and maintenance of the principles and laws cannot protect relatives and friends.

自重者然后人重，人轻者便是自轻。

Only those who value themselves can be valued by others. Those who are despised by others despise themselves first.

说长说短，宁说人长莫说短。

Talk more about the strengths of others rather than expose their weaknesses.

快意事过非快意，自古败名因败事。

When the thrill passes there is nothing to be happy about.
Reputation is ruined for bad deeds.

伤身事莫做，伤心话莫说。

Don't do things that are harmful to your health, and don't say
words that are not good for your mood.

小人肥口，君子肥身。

The villain only pursues appetite, but the gentleman takes self-
cultivation as his pursuit.

地不生无名之辈，天不生无路之人。

There must be a use for talents, and there must be a way out
for extremity.

一苗露水一苗草，一朝天子一朝臣。

One place's water and soil nurture its residents, the change of
authority changes the subordinates accordingly.

福满须防有祸，凶多料必无争。

Beware of misfortune when in happiness; no one comes to force
you when in dangers and difficulties.

但知江湖者，都是薄命人。

People who are street smart are most likely to meet a rough fate.

施恩施怨，宁施人恩莫施怨。

Give more kindness to others rather than giving them resentment.

自身不谨，扰乱四邻。

An unrestrained man will disrupt the lives of neighbors.

不怕三十而死，只怕死后无名。

Don't be afraid of dying early but be afraid of being nameless
after death.

育林养虎，虎大伤人。

Raising forests to raise tigers will hurt people eventually.

冤家抱头死，事要解交人。

Opponents cannot be reconciled without a middleman.

卷帘归乳燕，开扇出苍蝇。

The swallows come back when the curtains are rolled up; the
flies emerge when the windows are opened.

爱鼠常留饭，怜蛾灯罩纱。

Leave leftovers for rats; cover the lampshade for moths.

人命在天，物命在人。

The fate of man lies in the destiny of heaven, and the fate of
things is in the hands of man.

奸不通父母，贼不通地邻。

One cannot harm you by teaming up with your parents; thieves
cannot steal your belongings by teaming up with your neighbors.

盗贼多出赌博，人命常出奸情。

Gambling can be fatal; adultery too can lead to death.

治国信谗必杀忠臣，治家信谗必疏其亲。

Emperors cheated by slanderous talk kill loyal ministers;
patriarchs cheated by slanderous talk alienate relatives.

治国不用佞臣，治家不用佞妇。

Don't use traitorous officials to govern the country; don't use
flattering women to manage the family.

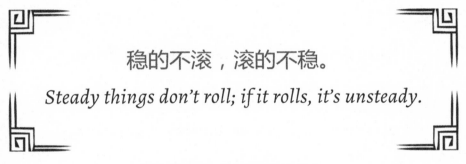

稳的不滚，滚的不稳。

Steady things don't roll; if it rolls, it's unsteady.

好臣一国之宝，好妇一家之珍。

Officials with good conduct are the treasure of a country,
and a wife with good conduct is the treasure of the family.

儿不嫌母丑，狗不嫌家贫。

The son does not dislike his mother for being ugly, and the dog
does not dislike his master for being poor.

君子千钱不计较，小人一钱恼人心。

The gentleman does not care about thousands of dollars, but the
villain will hound you for one cent.

人前显贵，闹里夺争。

If a person likes to show off how noble he is to others, he will often make a lot of noise in the fight for honor and money.

要知江湖深，一个不做声。

Keep your mouth shut to avoid troubles.

知止自当出妄想，安贫须是禁奢心。

Those who know that enough is enough are away from delusion; those who are content with poverty are away from luxury.

初入行业，三年事成。

It takes three years to master the skills of an industry.

初吃馒头，三年口生。

It takes three years to master the skills of making bread.

家无生活计，坐吃如山崩。

If a family does nothing to earn a living, a mountain of wealth will be exhausted.

家有良田万顷，不如薄艺在身。

It's better to have a skill than good fortune.

艺多不养家，食多嚼不赢。

Learn too many skills but not mastering one to support the family; eat too many breads but not digesting one makes you sick.

命中只有八合米，走遍天下不满升。

If you are destined to have only eight buckets of rice, you cannot make it ten even if you travel all over the world.

使心用心，反害自身。

The tricks you use will eventually turn around and hurt you.

国家无空地，世上无闲人。

If the country has no uncultivated farmland, then there will be no man idling around.

妙药难医怨逆病，混财不富穷命人。

Best medicine cannot cure a resentful man; a windfall cannot enrich a destined poor man.

耽误一年春，十年补不清。

Idle around for one spring and you cannot make it up even with ten years of hard work.

人能处处能，草能处处生。

Weeds can grow everywhere; talents can succeed everywhere.

会打三班鼓，也要几个人。

You cannot manage a three-man's work.

人不走不亲，水不打不浑。

People are close with constant communication; water is clear when it's calm.

只只船上有梢公，天子足下有贫亲。

Every boat has a helmsman, and every emperor has a poor relative.

三贫三富不到老，十年兴败多少人。

Wealth and poverty are not static for a lifetime, just look at how many people succeeded and failed within ten years.

人强不如货强，价高不如口便。

Good goods rather than slick sellers; negotiated prices rather than high prices.

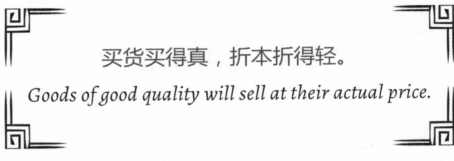

买货买得真，折本折得轻。

Goods of good quality will sell at their actual price.

不怕问到，只怕倒问。

Not afraid of being asked of price, but afraid of being asked about pricing.

会买买怕人，会卖卖怕人。

Those who are good at buying things will scare those who sell fakes; those who are good at selling things will scare those in the same industry.

既知莫望，不知莫向。

Don't complain if knowing the results; don't intervene if not knowing the story.

在一行，练一行。

Practice the skills since you are in the industry.

穷莫失志，富莫癫狂。

Don't lose ambition in poverty; don't be indulgent in abundance.

天欲令其灭亡，必先让其疯狂。

If God wants you to perish, he will want you to become
uncontrolled first.

梢长人胆大，梢短人心慌。

A talented man is full of confidence; an incompetent man is timid.

隔行莫贪利，久炼必成钢。

Don't be impatient when perfecting skills. Much refinement
makes the strongest steel.

瓶花虽好艳，相看不耐长。

The flowers in the bottle are beautiful at first sight but
overlooked when long in view.

早起三光，迟起三慌。

Get up early and things are done carefully. Wake up late and
things are done carelessly.

未来休指望，过去莫思量。

Don't have any expectations for tomorrow; don't have any
regrets for yesterday.

时来遇好友，病去遇良方。

Met a friend when not in difficulty; got a cure when not sick.

布得春风有夏雨，哈得秋风大家凉。

Spring breeze drives winter away; summer rain drives scorching away; autumn winds drive summer away.

晴带雨伞，饱带饥粮。

Bring an umbrella on sunny days, bring food even if you're full.

满壶全不响，半壶响叮当。

Full pots do not sound, half pots jingle.

久利之事莫为，众争之地莫往。

Don't do things that have always been profitable, don't go somewhere that everyone else is heading to.

老医迷旧疾，朽药误良方。

Experienced doctors get confused about treating diseases; rotten medicine harms a good prescription.

该在水中死，不在岸上亡。

If someone is destined to die in the water, one will not die on the shore.

舍财不如少取，施药不如传方。

It is better to take less than to give up money, and to give a prescription rather than take medicine.

燕子不进愁门，耗子不钻空仓。

Swallows do not build nests under the eaves where no one lives, and mice do not drill into warehouses empty of food.

苍蝇不叮无缝蛋，谣言不找谨慎人。

Flies don't bite uncracked eggs, and rumors don't infect cautious people.

人争一口气，佛争一炷香。

People fight for a breath, Buddha fights for a stick of incense.

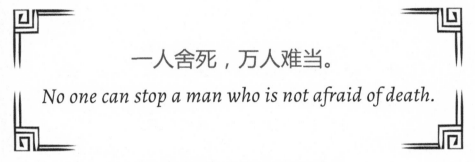

一人舍死，万人难当。

No one can stop a man who is not afraid of death.

倒了城墙丑了县官，打了梅香丑了姑娘。

Fallen, the walls of a county embarrassed the county official; bullied, the servant embarrassed his master.

门为小人而设，锁乃君子之防。

The door is for the villain, the lock is the gentleman's defense.

男子无志纯铁无钢，女子无志烂草无瓤。

Men without ambitions are like pure iron without steel, women without ambitions are like rotten grass without guidance for children.

好事他人未见讲，错处他偏说得长。

Good things are not talked of by others, but there are long conversations about wrong deeds.

生男欲得成龙犹恐成獐，生女欲得成凤犹恐成虎。

Hope the son to be a dragon and fear him becoming a coward; hope the daughter to be a phoenix but fear her becoming a tiger.

养男莫听狂言，养女莫叫离母。

Teach a boy not to listen to nonsense and teach a girl to listen to her mother.

男子失教必愚顽，女子失教定粗鲁。

Uneducated boys are ignorant; uneducated girls are rude.

生男莫教弓与弩，生女莫教歌与舞。

Don't teach boys about bows and crossbows, don't teach girls about singing and dancing.

学成弓弩沙场灾，学成歌舞为人妾。

A boy who learns the techniques of bow and crossbow will die on the battlefield; a girl who learns the techniques of singing and dancing will become someone's concubine.

财交者密，财尽者疏。

Everyone associates with a rich man and avoids a poor man.

少实胜虚，巧不如拙。

Less is better than nothing; clumsy is better than cunning.

硬弩弦先断，钢刀刃自伤。

The hard strings of crossbows always break first; the sharpest blades always hurt themselves.

舌咬只为揉，齿落皆因眶。

The tongue is bitten for talking while eating; the tooth falls out because of the socket.

贼名难受，龟名难当。

No one feels comfortable when called a thief; no one feels comfortable when called a tortoise.

婚姻论财，夫妻之道。

Marriage requires money as the prerequisite for the couple to live a good life.

色娇者亲，色衰者疏。

Beauty brings closeness; losing charm with years brings estrangement.

百战百胜不如无争，万言万中不如一默。

It is better to keep the peace than to win endless battles, and it is better to remain silent if the argument prevails.

有钱不置怨逆产，冤家宜解不宜结。

Don't buy an unlucky estate; don't keep a lasting enemy.

近朱者赤，近墨者黑。

A man is known by the company he keeps.

一个山头一只虎，恶龙难斗地头蛇。

Only one tiger lives on a hill; a dragon can hardly fight a local snake.

商贾买卖如施舍，买卖公平如积德。

Buying and selling between merchants is like charity. And fair business transactions are like doing good deeds.

天生一人，地生一穴。

God arranged for a person to be born, and there must be a place on earth where he will be buried in the future.

出门看天色，进门看脸色。

Look at the sky when you go out, look at the atmosphere when you come in.

家无三年之积不成其家，国无九年之积不成其国。

If a family does not have enough accumulated wealth to support it for three years, it cannot be said to be a family in the true sense; if a country does not have material reserves that can support its citizens for nine years, it cannot be said to be a true country.

男子有德便是才，女子无才便是德。

A man who is virtuous has a talent; a woman without talent has a virtue.

谦虚美德，过谦即诈。

Modesty is a virtue, but too modest is dishonest.

有钱难买子孙贤，女儿不请上门客。

Money alone cannot buy wisdom for the future generations;
girls should not be too courteous to guests knocking on the door.

男大当婚女大当嫁，不婚不嫁惹出笑话。

When a certain age is reached, a man will marry a wife, a
woman will marry a man; a man who does not marry is unfilial,
and a woman who does not marry will be gossiped about.

自己跌倒自己爬，望人扶持都是假。

Overcome difficulties on your own, and don't count on others
to help.

人不知己过，牛不知力大。

A person doesn't know his shortcomings, just like a cow doesn't
know its strength.

一家饱暖千家怨，一物不见赖千家。

All neighbors complain if one family is rich; all neighbors are
suspected if one family is robbed.

当面论人惹恨最大，是与不是随他说吧。

Discussing a man to his face makes him hold a grudge against
you, so let others do the talking.

谁人做得千年主，转眼流传八百家。

No one can be a master forever, and power has spread to many
others in a blink of an eye.

满载芝麻都漏了，还在水里捞油花！
Don't be penny-wise and pound-foolish!

皇帝坐北京，以理统天下。
The emperor lived in Beijing and ruled the world by reason.

五百年前共一家，不同祖宗也同华。
No matter what your surname is, you are all sons and daughters of China.

学堂大如官厅，人情大过王法。
The school is as big as the official hall, and the favor is greater than law.

找钱犹如针挑土，用钱犹如水推沙。
Saving money is like picking up soil with a needle, and wasting money is like pushing sand with waves.

害人之心不可有，防人之心不可无！
Harmfulness is not allowed, and defensiveness is necessary!

不愁无路，就怕不做。
I'm not afraid of not having roads, I'm afraid of not building roads.

思虑之害甚于酒色，日日劳力上床呼疾。
The harm caused by melancholy in the heart is far greater than the harm caused by indulging in alcohol. Working hard every day will make you feel weak and pained.

须向根头寻活计，莫从体面下功夫。

Find a way to the root, don't just scratch at the surface.

祸从口出，病从口入。

Misfortune comes out of the mouth; sickness comes from the mouth.

药补不如肉补，肉补不如养补。

Medicine is not as nourishing as meat tonic, and meat tonic is not as nourishing as meat.

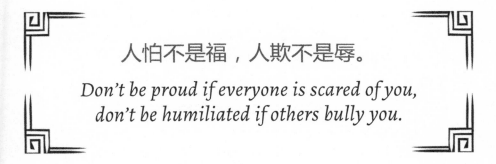

人怕不是福，人欺不是辱。

Don't be proud if everyone is scared of you,
don't be humiliated if others bully you.

能言不是真君子，善处方为大丈夫。

A slick man is not necessarily a gentleman; an honest man is a real gentleman.

为人莫犯法，犯法身无主。

Don't break the law or you will lose your freedom.

君子千里同舟，小人隔墙易宿。

A gentlemanly friend feels close even when distant; a villainous friend feels distant even when in the same room.

姊妹同肝胆，弟兄同骨肉。

The affection of sisters and brothers is like bones and blood.

慈母多误子，悍妇必欺夫。

A mother who spoils her children will delay their future; a wife who is powerful will bully her husband.

文钱逼死英雄汉，财不归身恰是无。

The want of a penny can drive the hero to death. A penny not in your pocket is worth nothing.

妻子如衣服，弟兄似手足。

Wife is like clothes, but brother is like bones and blood.

衣服补易新，手足断难续。

It's easy to wear new clothes but hard to live without bones and blood.

盗贼怨失主，不孝怨父母。

The thieves blame the owner, and unfilial children blame their parents.

一时劝人以口，百世劝人以书。

Persuade by words for one man but persuade by books for generations.

我不如人我无其福，人不如我我常知足。

If I'm not as good as others, then I don't have that destiny. If others are not as good as me, I should feel content with destiny.

捡金不忘失金人，三两黄铜四两福。

Once you have picked up the gold, you must immediately think of how anxious its owner is at its loss. It's just a couple of brass pieces in exchange for a couple of blessings.

因祸得福，求赌必输。

There are blessings in disguise in life, but gambling leads to failure.

一言而让他人之祸，一忿而折平生之福。

An improper word leads to a disaster; an impulse reduces the blessing of one's life.

天有不测风云，人有旦夕祸福。

The weather is as unpredictable as fate is.

不淫当斋，淡饱当肉。

Regard the absence of lust as a fast, and a light meal as a delicacy.

缓步当车，无祸当福。

Walking slowly is as good as driving a car. It is a blessing if nothing unfortunate happens.

男无良友不知己之有过，女无明镜不知面之精粗。

A man without a good friend doesn't know his shortcomings. A woman without a mirror doesn't know how her makeup looks.

事非亲做，不知难处。

If you don't do it yourself, you don't know how difficult it is.

十年易读举子，百年难淘江湖。

It's easy to get into Juren in ten years; it's harder to get a clear picture of the world in a hundred years.

积钱不如积德，闲坐不如看书。

It is better to do good deeds than to save money. It is better to read and study than to stay idle.

在家千日好，出门处处难。

Life outside is not as easy as at home.

树挪死，人挪活。

A tree dies if its place is changed; a man thrives if his environment is changed.

思量挑担苦，空手做是福。

Too many thoughts will drag you down like a burden. It is your blessing to create a career when you have nothing.

时来易借银千两，运去难赊酒半壶。

It's easy to borrow a fortune when you're in luck. If luck is gone, it's difficult to borrow even a penny.

天晴打过落雨铺，少时享过老来福。

The place where the sun is shining now has been rained upon in the past, and the young man can only enjoy his blessings when he is old.

与人方便自己方便，一家打墙两家好看。

Giving some convenience to others also brings convenience to oneself. One family demolished the wall, and both families were happy.

当面留一线，过后好相见。

Leave a glimmer of hope to avoid unnecessary embarrassment when you meet later.

入门掠虎易，开口告人难。

Hunting a tiger in mountains is easy; but asking for help from others is difficult.

手指要往内撇，家丑不可外传。

Fingers should always be turned inward, and skeletons in the cupboard shouldn't be gossiped about.

浪子出于祖无德，孝子出于前人贤。

Families have prodigal sons because their ancestors did not emphasize virtue, and families have filial children because their ancestors were wise.

货离乡贵，人离乡贱。

Products sell dearer further away from their place of production. People are held cheaper further away from their place of birth.

明人自断，愚人官断。

A wise man makes his own judgments; a stupid man relies on others to make judgments.

三员长者当官员，几个明人当知县。

The unwise all become the high-ranking officials.

人人依礼仪，天下不设官。

If everyone acted according to the etiquette, there would be no need for the judicial office.

人怕三见面，树怕一墨线。

A cunning man is exposed by face-to-face meetings; a crooked tree is exposed by measurement.

村夫硬似铁，光棍软如棉。

A man with a family will be full of energy; a man without a family will have no energy.

不是撑船手，怎敢拿篙竿！

If you are not a punter, how dare you pole?

天下礼仪无穷，一人知识有限。

The etiquette of the world is unlimited, but the knowledge of a man is limited.

一人不得二人计，宋江难结万人缘。

It's impossible for one man to make a plan with more than one; even Song Jiang can't be friends with everyone.

衙门钱，眼睛钱。

The money earned by serving in the government office may disappear in a twinkling of an eye.

金银到手非容易，用时方知来时难。

Gold and silver are not easy to come by.

靠山吃山，种田吃田。

Mountain villagers' food comes from mountains and farmers'
food comes from farming land.

田禾钱，千万年。

The money saved by farming and harvesting will be beyond the
reach of posterity for millions of years.

吃尽美味还是盐，穿尽绫罗还是棉。

*Salt seasons better than the costliest spice, and
cotton wears better than the finest silk.*

家有三亩田，不离衙门前，乡间无强汉，衙门就饿饭。

If the family had three acres of land, they could not live far away
from the government office. If there were no bullying incidents
in the countryside, the people in the government office would
have no food.

为人莫当官，当官皆一般。

Don't be an official for the officials are all the same.

换了你我去，恐比他还贪。

If you and I were to be in their positions, we might be greedier
than they are.

官吏清廉如修行，书差方便如行善。

The incorruptibility of officials is like cultivation, and the convenience given by secretaries is like doing good deeds.

一夫不耕，全家饿饭，一女不织，全家受寒。

If a man is not ploughing, the whole family will be starving, and if a woman is not weaving, the whole family will be shivering.

先讲断，后不乱，免得藕断丝不断。

Make the conditions clear in advance, and then there won't be a dispute.

听人劝，得一半。

He who is willing to accept others' advice is halfway to winning the battle.

不怕慢，只怕站。

A slow progress holds promise, but to stand stiff foreshadows failure.

逢快莫赶，逢贱莫懒。

Don't hurry when you are fast, and don't be lazy when you are cheap.

谋事在人，成事在天！

Man proposes, God disposes!

宁卖现二，莫卖赊三。

Better sell two now than three on credit.

长路人挑担，短路人赚钱。

A man carrying a load walking for a long distance did not sell his wares; he who walks a short distance sold his wares and made money.

赚钱往前算，折本往后算。

When people make money in business, they always think about the future, and if they lose money, they look back just as if they did not do business to achieve inner balance.

小小生意赚大钱，七十二行出状元。

A small business makes a lot of money. One may distinguish himself in any trade.

财来生我易，我去生财难。

Money is easy to make when luck comes and is difficult to make by mere efforts.

胆大不如胆小，心宽甚如屋宽。

It is better to be timid than bold, and a big heart is better than a big house.

妻贤何愁家不富，子孙何须受祖田。

A good wife makes a rich family; good children never live off of their heritage.

是儿不死，是财不散。

He who is destined to be his own son will not die; the money that is destined to belong to you will not go away.

十月滩头坐，一日下九滩。

If business opportunities do not come, we have to wait; if business opportunities come, we can benefit a hundredfold.

修起庙来鬼都老，拾得秤来姜卖完。

The ghosts are old when the temple is built. The ginger is sold out when the scales are picked up.

结交一人难上难，得罪一人一时间。

It is hard to make friends, but easy to offend one.

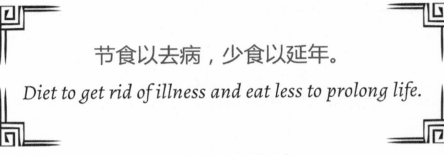

节食以去病，少食以延年。

Diet to get rid of illness and eat less to prolong life.

自己无运至，却怨世界难。

An unlucky man hates the difficult world.

借债经商，卖田还债。

Borrowing money to do business, selling farmland to pay debts.

赊钱起屋，卖屋还钱。

When you buy a house on credit, you sell it at the end to pay back the money.

不嫖莫转，不赌莫看。

Stay away from brothels and gambling dens.

豆腐多了是包水，梢公多了打烂船。

Too much water in tofu will lose its proper flavor; too many crests on boat will break sailing order.

无口过是，无眼过难。

He who keeps his mouth shut will get less trouble. He who blinds his eyes will get in trouble.

无身过易，无心过难。

If you stay out of trouble, you can keep yourself safe. If you do not have your own opinion, you will be in danger.

不会凫水怨河湾，不会犁田怨枷担。

I will not complain about the bend of the river, nor about the yoke of ploughing.

他马莫骑，他弓莫挽。

Don't ride another man's horse or draw another man's bow.

要知心腹事，但听口中言。

Hear what one says to know what he thinks.

宁在人前全不会，莫在人前会不全。

It is better to be modest before others than to show off.

打人莫打脸，骂人莫骂短。

Don't hit someone in the face, and don't scold someone for their shortcomings.

事非亲见，切莫乱谈。

Never talk until you see.

好言一句三冬暖，话不投机六月寒。

Kind words make you feel warm as in spring while evil words make you cold as in winter.

人上十口难盘，帐上万元难还。

It is difficult to interrogate a group of people; It is difficult to collect a debt over ten thousand yuan.

放债如施，收债如讨。

Lending money is like charity while collecting debt is like begging.

告状讨钱，海底摸盐。

Suing for debt is as difficult as it is to collect salt from the bottom of the sea.

衙门深似海，弊病大如天。

The government is as deep as the sea and its malady as great as the sky.

银钱莫欺骗，牛马不好变。

Don't cheat other people of their money, or you will become a beast in your afterlife.

好汉莫被人识破，看破不值半文钱。

All heroes are not necessarily perfect, but to keep their status in people's hearts, they must learn to keep up appearances.

狗咬对头人，雷打三世冤。

Some people deserve to be punished, and some people are wronged by misfortune.

高人求低易，低人求高难。

It is easy for a man in a higher position to seek a low position but is difficult for a man in a lower position to seek a high position.

人上一百，手艺齐全。

One hundred people have a complete skill set.

有钱就是男子汉，无钱就是汉子难。

Money makes a man a hero while poverty makes things difficult for him.

不卖香烧无剩钱，井水不打不满边。

Even if a person does not buy incense to burn, there is not much money left. Even if you do not go to fetch water from the well, the well will not be full.

事宽则园，太久则偏。

If the person who deals with the matter is broad-minded, then the matter will be handled very well, but if one stays in one thing for a long time, one will develop a prejudice.

难者不会，会者不难。

Those who can't don't know the method, while those who can, know.

生就木头造就船，砍的没得车的圆。

Even if there is talent, if not improved and used, eventually it will be reduced to mediocrity.

心不得满，事不得全。

There is no satisfaction for human's minds, and no perfection for things.

鸟飞不尽，话说不完。

Birds always fly, words never end.

人无喜色休开店，事不遂心莫怨天。

Don't open a shop if you do not have a happy smile. Don't complain about destiny if you do not succeed.

选婿莫选田园，选女莫选嫁奁。

Don't look for a husband for his property without looking at the person. Don't look for a wife for her dowry without looking at the person.

红颜女子多薄命，福人出在丑人边。

A beautiful woman is unfortunate while an ugly one is lucky.

人将礼义为先，树将花果为园。

We should put propriety first as a marker of maturity; a tree isn't productive until it blossoms and bears fruit.

贵人语少，贫子话多。

A noble man speaks little while a poor man talks too much.

临危许行善，过后心又变。

He promised to do good in times of danger, but then his
heart changed.

天意违可以人回，命早定可以心挽。

The will of God can be redeemed by human power. Fate can be
redeemed by the human heart.

强盗口内出赦书，君子口中无戏言。

From the mouth of a villain comes an amnesty, but from the
mouth of a noble man there is no joke.

快里须斟酌，耽误莫迟春。

If change comes too fast, we must carefully consider whether it
is necessary to modify and make trade-offs. If the best time to
act is delayed, it must be done within the time that there is still
hope for a change.

读过古华佗，不如见症多。

He who has read the ancients is no better than he who has seen
the diseases.

东屋未补西屋破，前帐未还后又拖。

The east house has not been repaired while the west house has
fallen into disrepair. The old debt goes unpaid while the new
debt is incurred.

今年又说明年富，待到明年差不多。

If we do things all our lives in anticipation of tomorrow, we are
bound to waste our time.

志不同己，不必强合。

Don't force people to cooperate when they have different ambitions.

莫道坐中安乐少，须知世上苦情多。

Don't complain when sitting in peace. There are too many people in the world who are suffering through difficult situations.

细处不断粗处断，黄梅不落青梅落。

A thin stick didn't break but a thick one did; a yellow plum didn't fall but a green one did.

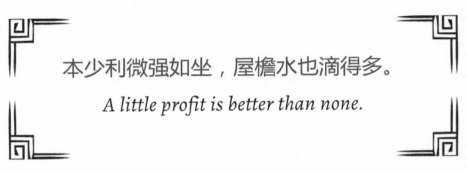

本少利微强如坐，屋檐水也滴得多。

A little profit is better than none.

勤俭持家富，谦恭受益多。

Frugality enriches the family; humility benefits the man.

见钱起意便是贼，顺手牵羊乃为盗。

If you see another's money and covet it for yourself, then you are already a thief. If you take away another's belongings when they are not looking, then you are already a robber.

栽树要栽松柏，结交要结君子。

If you plant a tree, plant a conifer; if you make friends, befriend a gentleman.

要做快活人，切莫寻烦恼。

To be happy is to not seek out troubles.

要做长寿人，莫做短命事。

If you want to live long, do not put yourself in danger.

要做有后人，莫做无后事。

If you want to have children, do not do evil things.

不经一事，不长一智。

No pain, no gain.

宁可无钱使，不可无行止。

Better to be without money than without exercise.

秀才不出门，能知天下事。

The scholar knows everything without leaving his home.

钱多不经用，儿多不耐死。

Too much money does not go far; too many children not a guarantee.

弟兄争财家不穷不止，妻妾争风夫不死不止。

Brothers' struggle for wealth will not end until the family is poor; wives' and concubines' struggle for husband will not end until the husband is dead.

男人有志，妇人有势。

A man is ambitious, a woman is powerful.

夫人死百将临门，将军死一卒不至。

When the wife of a ruler died, all officials came to offer their condolences. When the ruler himself died, no one came.

天旱误甲子，人穷误口齿。

When you are hungry and have nothing to wear, revenge will not be thought of for a while.

百岁无多日，光阴能几时。

A hundred years do not last long.

父母养其身，自己立其志。

Parents raise a man's body, and the man raises his own ambition.

待有余而济人，终无济人之日。

When you have no food left to help others, you find that day there is no one in need of your help.

待有闲而读书，终无读书之时。

When you have some spare time to read, you find that the best time to read has gone.

此书传后世，句句必精读，其中礼和义，奉劝告世人。

This book will be passed on to future generations; every sentence will be carefully read, advising the world to be polite and righteous.

勤奋读，苦发奋，走遍天涯如游刃。

Read this book carefully, and you will find that you're more skilled at all kinds of things in life.

【新增广贤文】

尊师以重道，爱众而亲仁。

We should respect teachers and emphasize humanistic morality and natural laws. We should treat all people with benevolence.

钱财如粪土，仁义值千金。

Money is like dung, and righteousness is worth more than gold.

饶人不是痴汉，痴汉不会饶人。

A fool will never forgive.

作事须循天理，出言要顺人心。

Behave in accordance with nature and speak in accordance with the people's hearts.

处富贵地，要矜持贫贱的痛痒，当少壮时，须体念衰老的辛酸。

To be restrained by the pain of poverty when rich; appreciate the bitterness of aging when young.

孝当竭力，非徒养身。

If you want to be filial to your parents, do your best; don't just take care of your parents' health.

鸦有反哺之孝，羊知跪乳之恩。

A crow has the filial duty of feeding back; lambs know the grace of kneeling to nurse.

打虎还要亲兄弟，出阵还须父子兵。

You need brothers to fight a tiger, and father and son fight better.

父子和而家不败，弟兄和而家不分。

When father and son are in harmony, the family is unbeaten;
when brothers are in harmony, the family is not divided.

知己知彼，将心比心。

Know yourself and know your enemy.

贪爱沉溺即苦海，利欲炽燃是火坑。

Indulging in love is like drowning in a sea of suffering, while
lust for profit burns like fire.

随时莫起趋时念，脱俗休存矫俗心。

Act according to the times but don't just go uncritically with
the flow; If you want to be a refined person, you can't have a
melodramatic mentality.

昼夜惜阴，夜坐惜灯。读书须用意，一字值千金。

Cherish the time to read. A word is worth a thousand dollars.

平生不作皱眉事，世上应无切齿人。

If you don't do bad things all your life, there will be no one who
hates you.

近水知鱼性，近山识鸟音。

He who lives near the water knows the habits of fish, and he
who lives near the hill knows the songs of birds.

美不美，乡中水；亲不亲，故乡人。

Water from hometown is the sweetest; friends from hometown are the best.

割不断的亲，离不开的邻。

A family member and a neighbor are inseparable.

但行好事，莫问前程。

Do good deeds, don't ask about the future.

钝鸟先飞，大器晚成。

The dullest bird flies first; great minds mature slowly.

一年之计在于春，一日之计在于寅。

A year's plan is made in the spring, and a day's plan is made in the morning.

一家之计在于和，一生之计在于勤。

Harmony is the key to a family; diligence is the key to a lifetime of success.

无病休嫌瘦，身安莫怨贫。

If you are not sick, don't be too thin. If you are healthy, don't complain about poverty.

岂能尽如人意，但求无愧人心。

The world cannot be completely in accordance with our own will, but we must be worthy of our own hearts.

偏听则暗，兼听则明。

Consider the opinions of all sides to correctly understand things; to believe only one side's words is bound to lead to error.

早把甘旨勤奉养，夕阳光阴不多时。

Serve your parents while they are still alive.

平日不作亏心事，半夜敲门心不惊。

I never do anything contrary to my conscience, and I am not afraid of a knock at the door at midnight.

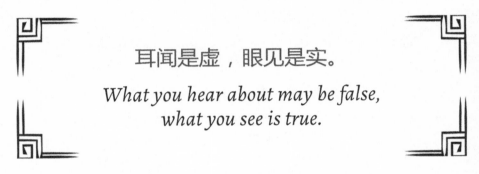

耳闻是虚，眼见是实。

*What you hear about may be false,
what you see is true.*

毋施小惠而伤大体，毋借公论而快私情。

Do not affect the interests of everyone because of small desires, and do not use public opinions to satisfy your own whims.

毋以己长而形人之短，毋因己拙而忌人之能。

Do not compare your strengths with others' weaknesses, and do not envy others' abilities because of your clumsiness.

汝惟不矜，天下莫与汝争能；汝惟不伐，天下莫与汝争功。

If you do not boast, there will be no one in the world to compete with you; If you are not arrogant, no one in the world will claim credit for your accomplishments.

明不伤察，直不过矫。

Shrewd and yet not overly exacting, upright and yet not overcompensating.

仁能善断，清能有容。

To have kindness of heart and wisdom of judgment; to have purity of heart and grace of toleration.

不自是而露才，不轻试以幸功。

Don't be arrogant and show off your talent, don't make a hasty attempt and hope for luck.

受享不逾分外，修持不减分中。

Material enjoyment should not be excessive and moral cultivation should not be meager.

肝肠煦若春风，虽囊乏一文，还怜茕独。

A benevolent man is compassionate even when he has no money.

气骨清如秋水，纵家徒四壁，终傲王公。

A man of character and integrity will not abase himself even if he is penniless.

得宠思辱，居安思危。

When a man gains honor, he should consider the possibility of disgrace; When there is peace, think of the possible danger.

许人一物，千金不移。

The promise once given is as good as thousands of bars of gold.

成名每在穷苦日，败事多因得意时。

Today's success is the result of yesterday's hard work; today's failure is the result of complacency.

博学而笃志，切问而近思。

To learn widely and to be faithful to one's purpose, to ask questions earnestly and to think often about the present.

惜钱休教子，护短莫从师。

Don't spare money in educating the young, and don't be too protective when the teachers discipline your kids.

须知孺子可教，勿谓童子何知。

Children are worth educating. Don't say they know anything.

静坐常思己过，闲谈莫论人非。

When sitting quietly, one should examine one's own faults, and when chatting with others, one should not talk about the faults of others.

三人同行，必有我师，择其善者而从，其不善者改之。

When three people are together, one could be my teacher. Follow the good and correct the bad.

狎昵恶少，久必受其累；屈志老成，急则可相依。

If you associate with evil boys, you will be dragged down by them over time. Connect with honorable people, and you can rely on them when things are urgent.

学不尚行，马牛而襟裾。

Learning without practice is like animals putting on the clothes of humans without changing their foolish natures.

同君一席话，胜读十年书。

One talk with a gentleman is worth ten years of reading.

道吾好者是吾贼，道吾恶者是吾师。

People who flatter me are hurting me, but people who criticize me are helping me.

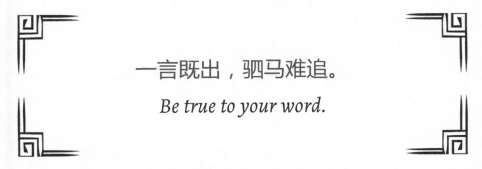

一言既出，驷马难追。

Be true to your word.

心口如一，童叟无欺。人有善念，天必佑之。

What you think and what you say should be the same, don't deceive even the old and the children. God bless a man with good intentions.

过则无惮改，独则毋自欺。

Don't be afraid to correct your mistakes. Even if you make a mistake when you are alone, you should take the initiative to correct it. Don't deceive yourself.

水至清，则无鱼；人至察，则无徒。

Clear water survives no fish.

宁可正而不足，不可斜而有余。

A virtuous man would rather be upright and poor than to rely on evil means to gain profits.

认真还自在，作假费功夫。

If you are serious and objective, you will be comfortable and calm; if you fake everything, you will waste time and energy.

是非朝朝有，不听自然无。

The words that stir up trouble come up every day; ignoring them is the best way to deal with them.

聪明逞尽，惹祸招灾。

Too much cleverness will lead to disaster.

富从升合起，贫因不算来。

Affluence is accumulated from daily life; poverty is often cause by careless living.

用人不宜刻，刻则思效者去；交友不宜滥，滥则贡谀者来。

If you're too mean, the people who work for you will leave. Don't make too many friends, for if there be too many, then people who are good at flattery will try to get at you.

乐不可极，乐极生哀；欲不可纵，纵欲成灾。

Do not overdo your happiness; when it is carried to its extreme, it turns to sorrow. Do not indulge desire; indulgence will lead to disaster.

言顾行，行顾言。

Think about what you can do when you say and think about what you can say when you do.

不作风波于世上，但留清白在人间。

Don't rock the boat. Be honest and keep a good reputation.

勿因群疑而阻独见，勿任己意而废人言。

Don't doubt your own opinions because others are skeptical. Don't be so stubborn that you don't value the opinions of others.

自处超然，处人蔼然。得意淡然，失意泰然。

Follow nature and be kind to others. Don't boast when you are successful, and don't cry out when you are frustrated.

由俭入奢易，由奢入俭难。

It is easy to go from frugality to luxury, but difficult to go from luxury to frugality.

枯木逢春犹再发，人无两度再少年。

Trees that have withered will sprout again in the next spring. But there is no way to make up for a wasted youth.

不学无术，读书便佳。

One who doesn't read knows nothing, one who reads is knowledgeable.

谦恭待人，忠厚传家。

Only by being humble and honest can we make ourselves and our children safe.

与治同道罔不兴，与乱同事罔不亡。

One takes on the color of one's company.

居身务期质朴，训子要有义方。

Cultivating one's morality requires naivete and naturalness,
and educating children requires them to behave morally.

富若不教子，钱谷必消灭。

If a rich family does not teach its offspring that, its money or
food is bound to be spent.

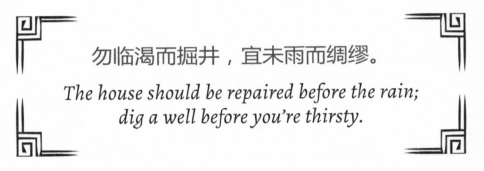

勿临渴而掘井，宜未雨而绸缪。

*The house should be repaired before the rain;
dig a well before you're thirsty.*

儿孙胜于我，要钱做甚么；儿孙不如我，要钱做甚么。

If my children are better than I am and make more money than
I do, I don't need to worry about money. If my children are not
as good as I am, I hope I don't have money for them to waste.

贵若不教子，衣冠受不长。

Powerful people can't enjoy their power for long if they don't
educate their offspring.

人无远虑，必有近忧。

Those who do not plan for the future will find trouble at
their doorstep.

酒虽养性还乱性，水能载舟亦覆舟。

Moderate drinking is good for the body while too much drinking cause trouble. Water can help a boat float, but it can sink it, too.

克己者，触事皆成药石；尤人者，启口即是戈矛。

People with good self-control are like a good medicine that helps others to cultivate morality and quit evil; people who often complain about the world talk like a spear pointing at others.

儿孙自有儿孙福，莫与儿孙做牛马。

The fortunes of children should be created by their own efforts, so don't do everything for them.

深山毕竟藏猛虎，大海终须纳细流。

Vast mountains are bound to hide tigers, and the sea will eventually take in small streams.

休向君子谄媚，君子原无私惠；休与小人为仇，小人自我对头。

Don't flatter the gentleman; the gentleman won't do favors for his own sake. Don't make enmity with those misbehaving villains; villains naturally have enemies.

登高必自卑，若涉远必自迩。

If you climb high, you will feel humble. If you travel far, you will feel shallow.

磨刀恨不利，刀利伤人指；求财恨不多，财多终累己。

I'm afraid it's not sharp enough when I sharpen my knife, but a with sharp knife it's easy to hurt my fingers. I'm afraid it's not enough when I pursue wealth, but too much pursuit of it will wear me out.

居视其所亲，达视其所举。

When a person is poor, see who he keeps company with. When a person is prominent, see how he selects his subordinates.

富视其所不为，贫视其所不取。

When a person is rich, see what he did with this wealth. When a person is poor, see what he didn't do.

知足常足，终身不辱；知止常止，终身不耻。

A contented person will not humiliate himself for indulgence for a lifetime; a restrained person knowing when to stop will never do shameful things all his life.

君子爱财，取之有道；小人放利，不顾天理。

Gentlemen love money, but they obtain it from proper channels; a villain gives out high interest loans and ignores the laws of God.

悖入亦悖出，害人终害己。

Property obtained by improper means will also be taken away by improper means, and in wanting to harm others you will eventually harm yourself.

身欲出樊笼外，心要在腔子里。

Though your body is eager to get out of the cage, your heart want to stay in.

勿偏信而为奸所欺，勿自任而为气所使。

Don't be deceived by treacherous people, don't be self-confident and driven by momentary mood.

使口不如自走，求人不如求己。

Better to act yourself than to give orders. Better to help yourself than to ask for help.

凡是自是，便少一是。

Someone feels self-righteous, then his advantages become less.

务下学而上达，毋舍近而趋远。

Explore the laws of things by learning and accumulating knowledge; don't ignore what is near to pursue what is far away.

学者如禾如稻，不学者如蒿如草。

People who like to learn are like seedlings; those who do not like to learn are like weeds.

处骨肉之变，宜从容不宜激烈；当家庭之衰，宜惕厉不宜委靡。

To deal with changes between relatives, the attitude must be calm and not too intense; when the family is declining, the attitude must be vigilant and not slack.

量入为出，凑少成多。

Plan expenditures based on income. Small daily savings can add up to a long-term fortune.

溪壑易填，人心难满。

The streams and river ditch are easy to fill, and people's desires are always endless.

用人与教人，二者却相反，用人取其长，教人责其短。

Using people and teaching people are opposites; use someone else's strengths and teach people on their shortcomings.

仕宦芳规清、慎、勤，饮食要诀缓、暖、软。

For the official, it is necessary to follow the principle of clean, cautious, and diligent, and their diets should be slow, suitable, and soft.

留心学到古人难，立脚怕随流俗转。

Even if you study hard, it is difficult to reach the ancient scholars' heights. In today's society, it is necessary to remind yourself not to be follow the easy path.

有短护短，更添一短。

Having a shortcoming is one thing but trying to conceal it is another even bigger shortcoming!

好问则裕，自用则小。

If you study hard and ask questions, you will learn more; if you are arrogant, you will learn less.

勿营华屋，勿谋良田。

Don't build a super-luxurious house, don't focus on buying fertile land; these are worldly things.

若争小可，便失大道。

If you blindly compete for small personal gains, it will harm your overall interests.

但能依本分，终须无烦恼。

As long as you are guarding yourself, you will not have trouble.

有言逆于汝心，必求诸道；有言逊于汝志，必求诸非道。

The words of others go against your feelings, and you must examine them from the moral perspective; the words of others accord with your feelings, and you must examine them from a different perspective.

吃得亏，坐一堆；要得好，大做小。

A person who is willing to accept losses can make many friends and win a network of resources; if a person wants to be affirmed by others, he must lower his posture and respect others.

志宜高而身宜下，胆欲大而心欲小。

A person must couple lofty ambitions with a humble attitude. Have the courage to forge ahead, but also pay attention to details.

唇亡齿必寒，教弛富难保。

If the lips are damaged, the teeth will catch cold, and if the education is weak, it will be difficult to keep wealth.

书中结良友，千载奇逢；门内产贤郎，一家活宝。

It is very precious to make good friends through reading, and it is very valuable to cultivate a talented and capable person in the family.

勿贪意外之财，勿饮过量之酒。

Don't be greedy for unexpected gains, and don't drink too much alcohol.

玩人丧德，玩物丧志。

You lose your morals if you tease people and lose your ambition if you tease things.

责善勿过高，当思其可从。

Don't teach others good deeds too strictly, make sure they can accept.

攻恶勿太严，要使其可受。

Don't reproach others for their faults too harshly but consider whether they can bear it.

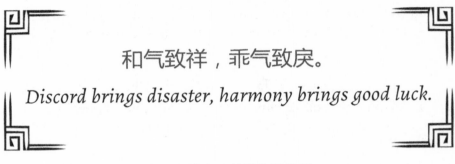

和气致祥，乖气致戾。

Discord brings disaster, harmony brings good luck.

进步便思退步，着手先图放手。

Before you move forward, you must first plan your retreat, and when you start to do something, you must first consider how you'll get away.

门内有君子，门外君子至；门内有小人，门外小人至。

I am a gentleman, and the friends I make are also gentlemen. I am a villain, and the friends I make are also villains.

家庭和睦，蔬食尽有余欢；骨肉乖违，珍馐亦减至味。

You can relish simple food in a harmonious home, while you'll have no appetite for delicacies in an inharmonious one.

趋炎虽暖，暖后更觉寒增；食蔗能甘，甘余更生苦趣。

Although it is warm near the fire it feels colder when you leave its side. Although eating sugar cane tastes sweet, other things will taste bitter eaten after it.

先学耐烦，切莫使气。

Learn to be patient first, and don't get angry.

性躁心粗，一生不济。

Impatient and rough-tempered, achievements will be rare in a lifetime.

得时莫夸能，不遇休妒世。

Don't boast about your abilities when you succeed, and don't be jealous when you don't.

物盛则必衰，有隆还有替。

When things prosper, they will inevitably decline, and prosperity will be replaced by desolation.

路径仄处，留一步与人行；滋味浓时，减三分让人嗜。

In the narrow roads, leave some space for others to walk by, and when there is something delicious, leave a part of it for others to taste.

持家要学小莫学大，门面一 弄阔了，后来难乎其继。

You must learn to be frugal in handling your household, and don't learn to be lavish. Once the facade becomes lavish, it becomes difficult to keep up appearances.

为人要学大莫学小，志气一卑污了，品格难乎其高。

It's better to learn from those above us than from those beneath us. Low ambitions don't help us to build high character.

三十不立，四十见恶，五十相将寻死路。

If you can't achieve your goals in adulthood, you will be despised and disgusted within a few years, and your life will be meaningless.

见怪不怪，怪乃自败。

Don't panic when you encounter a strange monster; it won't hurt you.

一正压百邪，少见必多怪。

A person who adheres to principles and thinks rationally will avoid all kinds of treacherous and illegal behaviors; and those with little knowledge will regard normal phenomena as strange.

君子之交淡以成，小人之交甘以坏。

Gentlemen's friendship is like pure water which stays wholesome for a long time. The acquaintance of the villain is like sweet drinks which often go bad within days.

爱人者，人恒爱。敬人者，人恒敬。

People who love others, others will always love back; people who respect others, others will always respect them.

损友敬而远，益友亲而敬。

Keep away from friends who might harm you and get closer to friends who are good for you.

善与人交，久而能敬。

A man who is good at communicating with people will receive people's respect.

过则相规，言而有信。

Friends will persuade each other when at fault and deliver on each other's promises.

一毫之恶，劝人莫作；一毫之善，与人方便。

Don't do even a small evil. Do others a favor even if it's small.

大事不糊涂，小事不渗漏。

Don't get confused when facing big challenges, and don't ignore small details.

木受绳则直，人受柬则圣。

The board will be made straight after being measured by the ink thread; the person who can accept other people's advice will become a saint.

素位而行，不尤不怨。

Act according to your usual status, do not blame others or yourself.

良药苦口利于病，忠言逆耳利于行。

Most of the good medicines are bitter, but they work for curing diseases; while the language that teaches people to be good is mostly unpleasant but works to help people cure their shortcomings.

智生识，识生断。当断不断，反受其乱。

A wise person has insight only when he deals with things decisively. If you aren't decisive when you should be, you will suffer the resulting chaos.

难合亦难分，易亲亦易散。

People with upright personality are difficult to make friends with but also difficult to lose as friends, and people who are easy to get close to are easy to approach and easy to lose.

传家二字耕与读，防家二字盗与奸。

Reading and farming can be regarded as family heirlooms and guard the family against evil and treacherous behaviors.

倾家二字淫与赌，守家二字勤与俭。

Prostitution and gambling will lead to bankruptcy, and only hard work and frugality can preserve the family business.

不汲汲于富贵，不戚戚于贫贱。

Don't worry about short-term poverty and low social status; don't pursue wealth improperly.

先达之人可尊也，不可比媚。

We should respect and learn from the senior with high morals and knowledge, but we should not compete with him indiscriminately.

权势之人可远也，不可侮慢。

Stay away from powerful people as much as possible, but don't be arrogant and don't offend them.

善有善报，恶有恶报，若有不报，日子未到。

People who do good or bad things will always get corresponding retribution sooner or later.

贤者不炫己之长，君子不夺人所好。

Virtuous people don't show off their abilities, and gentlemen don't take things that others love.

救既败之事，如驭临岩之马，休轻加一鞭。

Recovering and rescuing the things that have fallen is like driving a horse close to a cliff. Don't whip the horse carelessly to make it go nearer the edge.

图垂成之功，如挽上滩之舟，莫稍停一棹。

To grasp the victory that is out of reach, you must continue to do your best; when rowing a boat against the current, you must not stop to rest.

内藏精明，外示浑厚。

You have to hide shrewdness in your heart and look faithful and honest on surface.

恩宜先淡而浓，先浓后淡者，人忘其惠。

Blessings to others should go from weak to strong. If your generosity starts out strong, then gradually becomes weaker, people will quickly forget your former kindnesses.

威宜自严而宽，先宽后严者，人怨其酷。

To establish prestige, you must be strict and then tolerant. If you are tolerant and then severe, people will resent your coldness.

以积货财之心积学问，则盛德日新。

Those who accumulate knowledge with as much diligence as they accumulate wealth will be people with grand virtues.

安居饱食，天下太平。

Living in contentment, peace in the world.

以爱妻子之心爱父母，则孝行自笃。

Care for your parents as lovingly as you care for your wife and children, then your filial piety will be naturally profound.

事不终始，无务多业。

If one thing can't have a beginning and an end, don't take on other things.

学须静，才须学。

Learning comes with concentration, and talent comes from diligent learning.

非学无以广才，非静无以成学。

It is difficult to increase talents without studying, and it is difficult to achieve success without aspirations.

不患老而无成，只怕幼而不学。

It is not terrible for the old to do nothing; what is terrible is not to study when they are young.

富贵如刀兵戈矛，稍放纵便销膏靡骨而不知。

Wealth is as dangerous as weapons. A rich person can injure himself gravely if he indulges himself a little.

贫贱如针砭药石，一忧勤即砥节砺行而不觉。

Poverty is as helpful as needles for acupuncture and medicine for sickness. If worry makes you diligent, then poverty makes you super-diligent.

不矜细行，终累大德。

Regardless of the cultivation of the details, in the end it will hurt the big picture and lead to lifelong regrets.

亲戚不悦，无务外交。

If you can't get along with your relatives, you won't make friends outside.

民为邦本，本固邦宁。

Only when the people are the foundation of the country will the country will be peaceful.

临难勿苟免，临财勿苟得。

Don't get anything improperly in matters of property; and don't evade what you should face when facing crisis.

廉官可酌贪泉水，志士不受嗟来食。

As long as the incorruptible officials have a noble heart, they can boldly drink the water of the "greedy spring"; those of noble character do not accept humiliating alms.

谗言不可听，听之祸殃结。

Don't listen to slander. If you listen, it will cause disaster.

君听臣遭诛，父听子遭灭，夫妇听之离。

Slander causes the monarch to kill the loyal minister; causes the father to turn away from the son; causes the couple to divorce.

兄弟听之别，朋友听之疏，亲戚听之绝。

Slander separates brothers and alienates friends and relatives.

性天澄澈，即饥餐渴饮，无非康济身肠。

A person with a clear nature, even if life is difficult, sees that it is just to temper his body and will.

心地沉迷，纵演偈谈玄，总是播弄精魄。

A person addicted to fame and fortune, even if he pretends to be noble, is just tossing away his soul.

芝兰生于深林，不以无人而不芳。

Zhilan grows in the deep forest, giving off its fragrance even when there is no one to enjoy it.

君子修其道德，不为穷困而改节。

A virtuous person cultivates morality and establishes virtue and will not change his morality because of poverty.

ACKNOWLEDGEMENTS

We would like to give a special thank you to Jennifer Longworth for all her assistance with typesetting, book design, and setting up publishing through Amazon KDP; Alana Petrusiw and Derui Ma for their recommendations on improving the translation and preface; Dr. Ruthmita Rozul for her recommendation of a great book title; Riley Muir for her interview and featuring of our book in Yahoo Finance; and lastly to our many Linkedin / Weibo friends for helping with the book title and subtitle.

Conveyor Furnace

Great Price, Superior Performance, Built To Last

1. Multiple Zone Design
   - → Process temperature precisely meets ideal temperature profile
   - → Fast Heating & Cooling

2. Heater Choice: IR/FEC Ceramic Heater
   - → Highly efficient
   - → Fast thermal response
   - → Environmentally friendly
   - → Stable & precise temperature control
   - → Uniform temperature distribution (+-2C)

Our Furnaces

3. Atmosphere / Temperature Control
   - → Great insulation design
   - → Precise pressure control
   - → Low oxygen concentration

4. Multiple Model Fits All Applications:
   - → 6 series, 20+ models, 14 applications

More Products

Heat sinks,
Moly, Tungsten Alloys
& More Industrial Equipment

5. Highly Customized:
   - → Meets all your requirements
   - → Extendable belt design
   - → Build in Windows PC / retrievable temperature
     & speed profile

Furnace sales <info@torreyhillstech.com>
Torrey Hills Technologies, LLC
Telephone: (858) 558-6666
6370 Lusk Blvd # F111, San Diego, CA 92121

A LITTLE BIT OF EVERYTHING

FOR
EVERYONE

San Diego California

Who Are We

a leader in developing and delivering quality yet affordable materials, parts, and equipment for multiple industries. Core businesses: refractory metal heat sinks (CuW, CuMo, CMC, CPC), fabricated microelectronics packaging components, molybdenum, tungsten and alloy materials, along with furnace equipment for electronics and solar cell industry.

Ceramic RF, Microwave & Power Packages

More than 40 types of ceramic RF, microwave, and power packages with a maximum pulsed output power of up to 500W.Excellent thermal performance and microwave performance, suitable for silicon power transistor, LDMOS devices, GaAs, SiC and GaN power devices packaging.

Heat Sinks and More

Manufactured in a facility that specializes in R&D and production of high-tech electronic packaging materials heat sinks and shims. Our facility is the top in its field of electronic packaging materials with advanced material manufacture technologies, complete materials detective devices and modern management system. Our products are widely used in applications such as

heat sink, heat spreader, shim, laser diode submount, substrates, base plate, flange, chip carrier, optical bench, and more.

Tungsten, Moly and More

Pure metal and high density alloys of Tungsten, Molybdenum, and their composites are all available in the form of sheets, rods, bars, and machined parts.

Belt Furnaces

For firing, brazing, annealing, sintering, hardening, glass to metal seal, reflow soldering, epoxy curing, hermetic sealing, and LTCC applications.

CONTACT US
PH: 858-558-666
6370 LUSK BLVD F111
SAN DIEGO CA 92121

Heat Sinks

Refractory Metal Based Packaging Material

Cu/Mo/Cu Heat Sinks

Cu/Mo/Cu (CMC) is a sandwiched composite comprising a molybdenum core layer and two copper clad layers. It has adjustable CTE, high thermal conductivity, and high strength.

Cu/Mo/Cu	Density (g/cm3)	CTE (ppm/K)	Thermal Conductivity, W/m.K	
			In-Plane	Thru-Thickness
13:74:13	9.88	5.6	200	170
1:4:1	9.75	6.0	220	180
1:3:1	9.66	6.8	244	190
1:2:1	9.54	7.8	260	210
1:1:1	9.32	8.8	305	250

Cu/Mo70Cu/Cu (CPC) Heat Sinks

Cu/Mo70Cu/Cu (CPC) is a sandwiched composite similar to Cu/Mo/Cu comprising a Mo70-Cu alloy core layer and two copper clad layers. It has different CTEs in the X and the Y direction. Its thermal conductivity is higher than those of W/Cu, Mo/Cu, Cu/Mo/Cu and it is much cheaper.

Cu/Mo70Cu/Cu	Density (g/cm3)	CTE (ppm/K)		Thermal Conductivity (W/m.K)	
		X Direction	Y Direction	In-Plane	Thru-Thickness
1:4:1	9.46	7.2	9.0	340	300

F E A T U R E S

- Good thermal conductivity which is important to conduct the heat away from the IC's.
- Good hermeticity which is important to protect the immediate environment that the IC is in.
- Proper CTE to match that of IC's (Si, GaAs) and other packaging materials like alumina, BeO and AlN ceramic etc.
- Good mechanical strength to provide good mechanical protection to the IC's.
- Good machinability so that they can be formed to desired shapes.

Torrey Hills Technologies, LLC Tel (858) 558-6666
6370 Lusk Blvd., Suite F-111 Email sales@torreyhillstech.com
San Diego, CA 92121

Heat Sinks

Refractory Metal Based Packaging Material

The purpose of microelectronics packaging is to interconnect all active and passive components alike, and at the same time to protect the electronic devices from potential harms from environment like moisture, dust and gas and from other mechanical shocks. Microelectronics packaging has been steadily moving toward smaller form, lighter weight, lower cost, more functionalities, higher reliability and higher powers. Consequently the unit area heat dissipation is getting higher and higher. The excess heat, if not dissipated properly, increases the chip junction temperature and renders the chip unreliable.

Tungsten-Copper Heat Sinks

By adjusting the content of tungsten, we can have its coefficient of thermal expansion (CTE) designed to match those of materials such as ceramics (Al2O3, BeO), semiconductors (Si), and metals (Kovar), etc.

Type	Composition		Properties	
	Tungsten Content (wt %)	Density (g/cm3)	CTE (ppm/K)	Thermal Conductivity (W/m.K)
W90Cu	90 ± 1	17.0	6.5	180 - 190
W85Cu	85 ± 1	16.3	7.0	190 - 200
W80Cu	80 ± 1	15.6	8.3	200 - 210

Molybdenum-Copper Heat Sinks

Similar to W-Cu, CTE of Mo-Cu can also be tailored by adjusting the content of molybdenum. Mo-Cu is much lighter than W-Cu so that it is suitable for aeronautic and astronautic applications.

Type	Composition		Properties	
	Molybdenum Content (wt %)	Density (g/cm3)	CTE (ppm/K)	Thermal Conductivity (W/m.K)
Mo70Cu	70 ± 1	9.8	9.1	170 - 200
Mo60Cu	60 ± 1	9.66	10.3	210 - 250
Mo50Cu	50 ± 1	9.54	11.5	230 - 270

Torrey Hills Technologies, LLC
6370 Lusk Blvd., Suite F-111
San Diego, CA 92121

Tel (858) 558-6666
Email sales@torreyhillstech.com

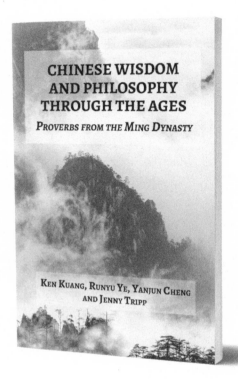

Made in United States
Orlando, FL
04 June 2022